RESTAURANT MARKETING FOUNDATIONS

PROVEN STRATEGIES TO ATTRACT CUSTOMERS, BUILD YOUR BRAND, AND BOOST RESTAURANT SUCCESS

RESTAURANT MARKETING BLUEPRINT

BOOK 1

JON NELSEN

DO SOCIAL SMARTER, LLC

marketing   est. 2017

CONTENTS

INTRODUCTION

The secret to thriving in the restaurant business often begins far from the kitchen. Picture this: a restaurant with perfectly cooked meals, an attentive staff, and a cozy atmosphere—but empty tables. Across town, another spot with average food and limited seating has a line out the door. The difference isn't the food or service—it's the marketing. The truth is, no matter how remarkable your dishes are, if people don't know about them—or worse, if they misunderstand what you offer—your restaurant may struggle to succeed. That's where the power of thoughtful, strategic marketing comes in.

Restaurants are more than just places to eat. They're spaces where people connect, celebrate, and seek comfort. But in today's crowded market, where new competitors emerge daily, standing out requires more than luck or guesswork. Marketing has become the lifeblood of a successful restaurant, influencing not just how customers find you, but how they feel about you before they even walk in. Danny Meyer, a celebrated restaurateur, once said that hospitality is a dialogue—a continuous exchange between staff, customers, and the world outside. Marketing is the loudest voice in that conversation, and getting it right means creating messages that resonate as much as the food itself.

At its core, marketing isn't just about ads or flashy campaigns. It's about understanding the people you serve. Imagine a family-owned diner that relies on word-of-mouth but notices a decline in weekend traffic. Instead of throwing money at a random promotion, they start listening—reading customer reviews, talking to regulars, and studying when people come in. They learn that a nearby restaurant's new loyalty program is pulling customers away. With this insight, the diner adapts, introducing its own rewards program tailored to its audience. The result? Not just a boost in sales, but a stronger connection with their community.

This book is built on one central idea: the restaurants that thrive are those that know their customers, align their efforts with clear goals, and present themselves consistently across every platform. It's not about quick fixes or gimmicks. It's about creating a foundation—one where every decision is grounded in strategy and purpose. Whether you're running a fast-casual café or a fine-dining establishment, the principles are the same. The way you tell your story, the channels you choose to share it, and the alignment between your brand and your operations are what set you apart.

Take branding, for instance. Strong restaurant brands like Chipotle or Shake Shack aren't accidents. Their success stems from consistent, recognizable messaging. Every ad, social media post, or storefront sign reflects their identity—whether it's Chipotle's commitment to fresh ingredients or Shake Shack's casual but elevated vibe. A small neighborhood restaurant can learn from these giants by committing to its own voice, whether that means celebrating its locally sourced menu or the history of its family recipes. Consistency isn't about copying big brands— it's about being unmistakably you.

Of course, marketing isn't just about creating; it's about measuring, too. Many restaurants make the mistake of assuming their efforts are working because they feel busy. But without data, you're guessing. If a bakery posts Instagram photos daily but sees no spike in foot traffic, the problem might not be the content, but the timing or the audience. By using tools like Google Analytics or studying customer trends, that same bakery could discover that email campaigns reach their audience more effectively. Marketing thrives on reflection and refinement, and the willingness to adapt often separates successful businesses from those stuck spinning their wheels.

Ultimately, this book isn't about teaching you every single marketing tactic—it's about giving you the tools to think strategically, so every campaign, menu redesign, or promotion works together toward your goals. Marketing isn't magic; it's method. And when it's done right, it can transform not just your business, but the way your customers experience your restaurant. Let's start building something unforgettable together.

Turn casual diners into loyal fans with Do Social Smarter's proven system to grow your customer base, boost reviews, and drive foot traffic effortlessly.

Visit DoSocialSmarter.com today and discover how to keep your seats full and your competition behind.

CHAPTER 1
UNDERSTANDING THE BASICS OF RESTAURANT MARKETING

HOW A SOLID FOUNDATION SETS THE STAGE FOR SUCCESS

Restaurants often rely on more than just good food and service to succeed. Marketing, though sometimes overlooked, plays a vital role in drawing in diners, keeping them coming back, and ensuring long-term growth. A well-thought-out marketing plan doesn't just attract attention; it builds trust, showcases what makes a restaurant unique, and creates lasting connections with customers. Whether it's about understanding your audience or setting goals that lead to real results, laying the groundwork for effective marketing is as important as perfecting your menu or service.

Marketing for restaurants starts with answering a simple but powerful question: "Why should someone choose you?" The answer lies in understanding your strengths and making sure your audience knows them, too. From identifying the specific types of customers you want to serve to crafting a clear message about what makes your establishment stand out, these foundational steps set the stage for every other marketing effort. Without a clear direction, even the best campaigns can fall flat, leaving potential opportunities untapped.

At its core, restaurant marketing is about creating a promise and delivering on it. This promise begins with defining who you serve, what they value, and how you meet their needs better than anyone else. These concepts form your brand and guide how you communicate with your customers. Establishing this connection ensures that every promotion, menu update, or event resonates with the people most likely to support your business.

Goals are another cornerstone of effective marketing. They help focus your efforts and measure what works. A restaurant without clear objectives may find itself trying random strategies, hoping for results. On the other hand, setting specific, measurable goals makes it easier to see progress and fine-tune your approach. When every decision ties back to a clear purpose, marketing becomes more than just an expense—it becomes a tool for growth.

With these basics in place, the path to successful restaurant marketing becomes much clearer. It's about starting with a strong foundation and using it to build meaningful relationships with your customers. By focusing on these key ideas, you're not just preparing to market your restaurant; you're setting it up to thrive.

The Role of Marketing in Restaurant Success

In 1985, Danny Meyer opened Union Square Cafe in New York City, an unassuming restaurant that would go on to redefine what it means to market a dining experience. Meyer didn't rely on flashy ads or big-budget promotions; his secret was "enlightened hospitality." This idea, simple yet profound, focuses on creating a culture where employees feel valued and empowered. Meyer believed that when employees are happy, they extend that warmth and care to customers, transforming a meal into an unforgettable experience. His approach highlights a critical lesson: marketing begins from the inside out.

Restaurants often think of marketing as something external—

social media posts, ads, or promotions. But at its core, marketing is about **building relationships and trust**, and that starts with how a business operates internally. When employees feel pride in their work and alignment with the restaurant's goals, this energy is naturally communicated to customers. A server who truly believes in the dishes they're recommending or a host who greets every guest warmly is engaging in the most effective marketing of all. **Marketing, at its best, is a seamless integration of culture, service, and strategy.**

Aligning marketing with broader business goals is another essential piece of the puzzle. Imagine a restaurant owner whose primary goal is to increase dinner sales, but their marketing focuses solely on lunchtime specials. Without clear alignment, the marketing effort feels disjointed and wastes valuable resources. Every marketing decision should reflect the restaurant's priorities, whether it's increasing foot traffic during specific hours, launching a new menu item, or promoting private dining events. **Clear goals act as a compass, ensuring marketing efforts point in the right direction and contribute to measurable success.**

However, many restaurants fall into common traps that undermine their marketing potential. One of the most frequent mistakes is failing to define a unique identity. When a restaurant's branding is vague or inconsistent, it becomes forgettable in the minds of customers. If diners can't answer the question, "What makes this place special?" they are less likely to return. **A restaurant's identity should be clear and consistent, from the tone of its social media posts to the way its menu is designed.**

Another common pitfall is neglecting the power of customer feedback. Ignoring or mishandling reviews—whether positive or negative—can erode trust and limit growth. Customers want to feel heard, and responding thoughtfully to feedback shows that the restaurant values their input. **Engaging with reviews is** more than damage control; it's an opportunity to strengthen relationships and demonstrate accountability.

Finally, many restaurants underestimate the importance of staff training as a marketing tool. Employees are the most direct representatives of a brand, and their ability to communicate the restaurant's story can make or break the guest experience. A server who can confidently describe the inspiration behind a dish or recommend a perfect wine pairing elevates the meal and reinforces the brand's image. **Investing in staff education is not just a behind-the-scenes effort—it's a key part of the restaurant's marketing strategy.**

The role of marketing in restaurant success is expansive, touching every aspect of the business, from how employees are treated to the clarity of the restaurant's goals. By adopting principles like enlightened hospitality and ensuring every decision aligns with broader objectives, restaurants can create a marketing strategy that feels effortless yet deeply impactful. And when a restaurant avoids common pitfalls, it lays the foundation for long-term growth and meaningful connections with its customers.

Identifying Your Target Audience

Have you ever wondered why some restaurants seem to thrive effortlessly, while others struggle to fill their tables? The answer often lies in their understanding—or lack thereof—of their audience. Knowing who your customers are isn't just a helpful insight; it's the foundation of every successful marketing strategy. Without this clarity, even the best campaigns can miss the mark, wasting resources and leaving potential diners unimpressed.

Defining your audience means going beyond vague categories like "families" or "young professionals." It's about identifying specific **demographics, preferences, and behaviors** that drive their decisions. For example, are your customers more likely to crave a quick weekday lunch or a relaxed weekend dinner? Do they value locally sourced ingredients, or are they drawn to budget-friendly options? By narrowing down these details, you can craft messages that resonate deeply and authentically. **People are far more likely to respond to marketing that feels personalized and relevant to their needs.**

To begin, focus on collecting actionable data. Start by examining your current customer base. Tools like point-of-sale systems and online reservation platforms can provide valuable insights into who is already dining at your restaurant. Look for patterns in the data—repeat visits, peak dining times, and most-ordered dishes. This information paints a picture of your loyal patrons and can help you understand what keeps them coming back. **The better you know your customers, the easier it is to find more just like them.**

Market research techniques add depth to these observations. Surveys, both online and in-person, allow you to gather direct feedback about customer preferences. Questions should be simple yet revealing: What do they love most about your restaurant? How did they hear about you? What changes or additions would make them visit more often? Social media polls and online review platforms also provide unfiltered opinions that can guide your understanding. **These tools turn customer voices into actionable insights.**

Once you've identified your audience, you can use tools to refine your strategies further. Google Analytics, for instance, helps track the behavior of visitors to your website, offering clues about what potential customers value. Social media analytics reveal who is engaging with your posts, their age, location, and even interests. With these resources, you can ensure your messaging reaches the right people in the right places.

Understanding behaviors is just as critical as analyzing demographics. A study cited in *Restaurant Marketing for Owners and Managers* revealed that customers are more likely to dine out based on emotional triggers—celebrations, convenience, or a desire for connection. Knowing this allows you to position your restaurant as the go-to place for these moments. For instance, marketing your space as "perfect for anniversaries" or offering specials that highlight convenience can attract the right crowd.

Without this level of focus, restaurants often fall into the trap of marketing to everyone and appealing to no one. This scatter-shot approach dilutes your message and wastes resources. By contrast, targeted marketing feels personal and intentional, which creates stronger connections. When your audience feels seen and understood, they're more likely to choose your restaurant over competitors.

Defining your target audience doesn't just guide your marketing; it aligns your entire business. It influences your menu choices, decor, and even staff training. By tailoring every aspect of your restaurant to the needs of your ideal customer, you create a cohesive experience that keeps people coming back. **Every successful decision begins with a deep understanding of the people you aim to serve.**

Understanding your audience isn't a one-time task. It's a continuous process of listening, observing, and adapting. As trends change and customer preferences evolve, so should your strategies. With the right tools and a clear focus, you can stay ahead of the curve, ensuring your restaurant remains a favorite in the eyes of your ideal diners.

Crafting a Unique Value Proposition

"People don't buy what you do; they buy why you do it." This quote from Simon Sinek, a thought leader in marketing, encapsulates the essence of crafting a unique value proposition. In the crowded world of restaurants, where countless establishments offer delicious food and warm ambiance, it's the "why" behind your restaurant that captures attention and loyalty. Your value proposition is the heartbeat of your business—the clear, compelling reason diners choose you over the competition.

Creating a unique value proposition begins with understanding what sets your restaurant apart. It's not enough to claim great food and excellent service; these are expectations, not differentiators. The key lies in **uncovering the distinct elements of your restaurant's identity**. Are you the only place in town offering authentic Neapolitan pizza baked in a wood-fired oven? Do you source all your ingredients locally and share the stories behind them? Maybe your establishment is known for crafting a welcoming environment where families can relax and celebrate together. Whatever your unique qualities are, they should be clear and memorable.

To define your value proposition, start with your strengths. Consider what customers frequently praise about your restaurant. Pay attention to online reviews, surveys, and face-to-face feedback. Look for patterns in the compliments—do people rave about your creative cocktails, your staff's attentiveness, or the vibe of your space? **This feedback reveals what customers already value, forming the foundation of your proposition.**

Next, think about your audience. An effective value proposition speaks directly to the desires and needs of the people you serve. For example, if you cater to health-conscious diners, emphasize how your dishes balance flavor and nutrition. If your restaurant thrives on its late-night crowd, highlight your lively atmosphere and extended hours. **A strong proposition bridges what you offer with what your audience craves.**

With your unique qualities and audience in mind, refine your message into a single, impactful statement. This statement should clearly communicate the benefit your restaurant provides, why it matters, and how it stands out. Keep it concise and direct—your value proposition isn't a tagline, but it should be easy for anyone to understand and remember. For instance, "Farm-to-table dining with a story in every dish" or "Where modern flavors meet old-world hospitality." **These statements give customers an immediate sense of what to expect and why they should care.**

Examples from the industry show how powerful a well-crafted value proposition can be. Chipotle, for instance, built its brand on "Food with Integrity," highlighting its commitment to sustainably sourced ingredients. This clear promise resonated with a growing audience of environmentally conscious diners. On a smaller scale, a local café might market itself as "Your home away from home, where every cup comes with a smile," emphasizing comfort and community. These propositions succeed because they align with their audiences' values and create a distinct identity.

Finally, test your value proposition. Share it with trusted team members, loyal customers, and even friends outside the industry. Does it resonate? Does it clearly differentiate your restaurant? Adjust your statement based on feedback, ensuring it feels authentic and specific. Once finalized, make it the cornerstone of your marketing efforts. **Your value proposition should guide every menu update, social media post, and campaign. When consistency reinforces your message, it becomes part of how customers define your brand.**

Crafting a unique value proposition is a process that requires thought, input, and refinement. Yet, it's one of the most important steps in building a strong, sustainable restaurant brand. By pinpointing what makes you unique and communicating it clearly, you create a lasting impression that keeps diners coming back for more.

Setting Measurable Marketing Goals

"Goals are dreams with deadlines," the legendary Napoleon Hill once said, and nowhere is this more evident than in the competitive world of restaurant marketing. Without clear, measurable goals, even the best ideas can falter, leading to wasted time, missed opportunities, and underwhelming results. Goals not only define what success looks like but also offer a roadmap for how to get there. They turn vague aspirations into actionable steps, providing clarity and focus in a crowded and fast-moving industry.

The concept of SMART goals—specific, measurable, achievable, relevant, and time-bound—is a cornerstone of effective planning. Imagine a restaurant aiming to "get more customers." While the intention is good, the lack of clarity makes it impossible to act upon. Compare that to a goal like, "Increase weekday lunch reservations by 20% within three months using targeted email campaigns." This refined approach highlights exactly what needs to happen and sets a deadline for achieving it. **When goals are clear and structured, they inspire confidence and provide direction.**

Aligning marketing goals with business priorities is equally vital. A fine dining restaurant might prioritize increasing dinner reservations, while a casual café may aim to boost coffee sales during morning hours. Marketing strategies that stray from these objectives, no matter how creative, fail to serve the restaurant's broader mission. For example, focusing solely on Instagram followers might generate attention but won't necessarily translate to revenue unless tied to a goal like promoting a seasonal menu or an event. **Marketing should never exist in a vacuum; it must support the larger vision of the business.**

Establishing actionable marketing goals begins with understanding your starting point. Data is key here. Use analytics tools to track performance metrics, such as website traffic, online reservations, and customer feedback. If you notice that your happy hour promotions receive limited engagement on social media, set a goal to increase click-through rates by 15% in six weeks by improving ad copy or investing in targeted ads. **Actionable goals are built on insights that highlight opportunities for growth.**

Successful examples abound in the restaurant world. A family-owned Italian restaurant might set a goal to increase repeat visits by 25% over six months by launching a loyalty program. This strategy ties directly to a measurable outcome and aligns with the business's priority of fostering customer loyalty. Alternatively, a new fusion eatery might aim to increase brand awareness by securing 10 media mentions within three months through outreach to local food bloggers. In both cases, the goals are specific and tailored to the restaurant's unique needs.

The importance of regular progress tracking cannot be overstated. A goal that sits untouched is as good as forgotten. Break larger goals into smaller milestones, and review them weekly or monthly. For instance, if your objective is to increase email open rates to 30% within three months, analyze the performance of individual campaigns to identify trends and areas for improvement. **Tracking progress not only keeps you accountable but also allows for timely adjustments that improve results.**

Setting measurable goals isn't just about hitting targets; it's about fostering a culture of continuous improvement. When every team member understands the goals and how their efforts contribute, they become more invested in the restaurant's success. Staff might even bring fresh ideas to the table, such as offering personalized recommendations to diners or brainstorming ways to increase social media engagement. **Goals inspire action, innovation, and collaboration, all of which are crucial to thriving in today's restaurant landscape.**

By grounding your marketing in SMART goals and ensuring they align with your business priorities, you create a system that drives results and keeps your team focused. These goals don't just measure success; they fuel it, turning every marketing effort into a step toward growth and sustainability.

Application of Techniques: Foundations of Restaurant Marketing Success

Restaurant marketing is an intricate balance of knowing your audience, defining your identity, and setting measurable goals. The chapter provides actionable frameworks that transform abstract ideas into real-world practices. Let's explore how these techniques can be implemented effectively.

Building Relationships Through Marketing Marketing isn't merely about external promotions; it starts with internal culture. Applying Danny Meyer's concept of "enlightened hospitality," restaurants can focus on making employees feel valued. Empowering staff with knowledge about the menu and the restaurant's story encourages them to act as ambassadors. For example, training servers to confidently share the origin of dishes or recommend pairings connects with customers on a deeper level, reinforcing the restaurant's identity.

Defining Your Audience Tools like point-of-sale systems or reservation platforms help identify patterns in customer behavior. A fine-dining restaurant could notice a drop in weekday reservations and target corporate professionals with lunch specials tailored to their preferences. Conducting surveys or leveraging social media polls reveals what resonates most, enabling restaurants to refine offerings or marketing campaigns based on specific audience desires.

Crafting a Unique Value Proposition Your value proposition is your restaurant's promise to its customers. Define what makes your restaurant unique by analyzing customer feedback. If diners frequently compliment your seasonal menu, center your value proposition on "Farm-to-Table Dining with Local Flavors." Integrate this into your marketing campaigns, from social media captions to email newsletters, ensuring consistency in communicating what makes you special.

Setting and Measuring Goals The SMART framework ensures marketing goals are actionable and aligned with business priorities. For example, a coffee shop aiming to increase foot traffic can set a SMART goal to "boost morning sales by 15% within three months through digital ads and loyalty cards." Analytics tools track campaign performance, while weekly reviews keep the team focused on adjustments if goals fall short.

Action Item Checklist

Enhance Employee Engagement:

- Conduct a staff meeting to explain your restaurant's brand values.
- Train employees to describe the inspiration behind menu items confidently.
- Implement a recognition program to celebrate employees who deliver exceptional guest experiences.

Identify and Analyze Your Audience:

- Review sales data and identify peak dining hours, customer demographics, and favorite dishes.
- Conduct customer surveys asking about dining habits, preferences, and suggestions.
- Use Google Analytics to monitor website traffic and understand visitor behavior.

Create a Unique Value Proposition:

- List three elements that make your restaurant unique (e.g., ambiance, menu, or service).
- Write a concise statement that highlights your distinct qualities.
- Test the statement with loyal customers or team members for feedback.

Set SMART Goals:

- Define one business priority (e.g., increasing dinner reservations).
- Create a specific, measurable goal (e.g., "Increase dinner reservations by 20% within three months by running targeted ads").
- Break down the goal into smaller tasks and assign them to team members.

Track Progress:

- Use analytics tools to monitor the effectiveness of campaigns (e.g., open rates for email newsletters).
- Schedule weekly reviews to evaluate progress and identify areas for improvement.
- Adjust strategies based on data insights, such as shifting ad budgets to higher-performing platforms.

Resource List

Tools:

- **Google Analytics**: Tracks website traffic and user behavior, helping refine digital campaigns.
- **Social Media Analytics (Facebook Insights, Instagram Analytics)**: Provides engagement metrics to identify what content resonates with followers.
- **POS Systems (e.g., Toast, Square)**: Analyzes customer purchasing patterns and sales trends.

Books and Reading Material:

- *Setting the Table* by Danny Meyer: Explores the concept of enlightened hospitality and its impact on restaurant success.
- *Restaurant Success by the Numbers* by Roger Fields: Offers practical advice on managing restaurant operations and marketing effectively.

Additional Resources:

- **Coursera Course: Restaurant Revenue Management**: Learn how to maximize restaurant profitability through strategic marketing and customer segmentation.
- **Local Chamber of Commerce**: Provides insights into community demographics and networking opportunities to build local awareness.
- **Online Forums (e.g., Restaurant Business Online)**: A space to discuss challenges and strategies with other restaurant professionals.

Closing Insights

By applying the lessons in this chapter, restaurants can create marketing strategies that are not only compelling but also deeply aligned with their brand and audience. From defining your unique value to measuring progress with precision, each step builds a foundation for sustained growth and meaningful customer connections. These strategies, when consistently executed, ensure that marketing evolves into a vital part of your restaurant's long-term success.

CHAPTER 2
BUILDING A MEMORABLE RESTAURANT BRAND

STAND OUT IN A CROWDED MARKET WITH A STRONG BRAND IDENTITY

Every great restaurant has a story, and your brand is how that story comes to life. It's not just a logo or a catchy name; it's the feeling people get when they walk through your doors, open your menu, or see your posts online. Branding is what makes your restaurant more than a place to eat—it's what makes it memorable. In a crowded market where countless establishments offer good food and friendly service, a strong brand identity is what sets you apart.

Think about your favorite restaurants. Chances are, they're not just places to grab a bite; they're experiences. Maybe it's the cozy corner café where every detail, from the cups to the playlist, makes you feel at home. Or perhaps it's the sleek bistro that exudes sophistication with every dish and design choice. These aren't accidents. They're the result of thoughtful branding, where every element works together to tell a cohesive story.

A well-crafted brand does more than attract customers—it creates loyalty. When people identify with your restaurant's values, style, or even just the way it makes them feel, they're more likely to keep coming back. But building that connection doesn't happen by chance. It starts with understanding who you are as a business, what makes you unique, and how to communicate that consistently across every touchpoint. From the colors you choose to the tone of your social media posts, every decision contributes to the bigger picture.

Branding also plays a key role in setting expectations. When done well, it tells customers what kind of experience they can expect before they ever walk in the door. If your restaurant is known for its fun, family-friendly atmosphere, your branding should reflect that. If it's an upscale spot for special occasions, that should come through loud and clear. A mismatch between what people see and what they experience can lead to confusion —and missed opportunities.

But branding isn't just about the external image; it's about the culture you build within your business. A clear and strong brand gives your team something to rally around, helping them understand their role in creating a memorable experience. When your staff embodies your brand values, it creates an authentic connection with customers that no advertising budget can match.

The foundation of a successful restaurant brand lies in clarity, consistency, and authenticity. By understanding the elements that make up your identity and how they work together, you can build a brand that not only stands out but leaves a lasting impression. It's not just about being seen—it's about being remembered.

What Is Restaurant Branding?

When you hear the name of a favorite restaurant, what's the first thing that comes to mind? Maybe it's the look of their logo, the atmosphere of their dining room, or the way their menu seems to match exactly what you're craving. That instant recognition and connection are not accidental—they're the result of effective branding. In the world of hospitality, where every detail matters, branding is the invisible thread that ties together every element of a restaurant's identity, shaping how customers perceive and remember it.

Branding in the restaurant industry is more than just a visual identity; it's the promise you make to your customers. It conveys who you are, what you stand for, and what people can expect every time they visit. A strong brand doesn't just tell a story—it invites customers to become part of it. This is especially important in hospitality, where the experience is often as important as the product itself. A well-branded restaurant can turn a casual meal into an event, making diners feel connected and valued.

To understand branding, it's helpful to break it down into its core components. **The first and most visible aspect is the visual identity**, which includes the logo, color scheme, typography, and other design elements. These are the building blocks of how customers recognize your brand, both in-person and online. But branding runs deeper than visuals. **The second element is the restaurant's voice and tone**, reflected in how it communicates through menus, social media, and customer interactions. A playful taco shop and a high-end steakhouse may both offer excellent food, but the way they speak to their audience is what defines their personality.

Another essential component is the emotional connection a brand creates. Research in consumer psychology shows that customers often choose brands based on how they make them feel, rather than what they offer. A restaurant that consistently delivers warm service, an inviting atmosphere, or a sense of adventure builds trust and loyalty over time. This connection is where branding has the most profound impact: it makes your restaurant memorable.

Branding shapes how customers perceive your restaurant, often before they ever set foot inside. Consider the way high-end restaurants use minimalistic design and refined language to signal sophistication and exclusivity. Meanwhile, a casual diner might use bold colors, playful typography, and friendly phrases to create an approachable, family-friendly vibe. These choices don't just reflect the restaurant's personality—they actively influence how customers feel about their potential experience.

The importance of branding becomes even clearer when you consider how competitive the restaurant industry is. Without a clear and cohesive brand, a restaurant risks blending into the crowd, losing the chance to make a lasting impression. On the other hand, a well-branded establishment becomes recognizable, even iconic, turning casual diners into loyal patrons. When every element of your brand aligns with your mission and audience, it creates an authenticity that resonates far beyond the food you serve.

Building a restaurant brand takes effort, but it starts with one simple question: what do you want people to think, feel, and remember when they hear your name? Answering that question with clarity and intention allows you to shape every aspect of your restaurant's identity, creating a brand that stands out, builds trust, and keeps customers coming back.

Creating a Visual Identity

Have you ever noticed how the mere sight of a golden arch or the distinct red-and-white stripes of a fast-food logo can trigger cravings or memories? That is the power of a well-designed visual identity. In the restaurant world, a strong visual identity does more than attract attention—it communicates what your brand stands for, creating an emotional connection with customers before they even walk through the door.

A restaurant's visual identity starts with its logo, which serves as the face of the brand. A logo should be instantly recognizable, aligning with the restaurant's personality and core values. A sleek, minimalistic design works well for upscale dining, while playful or vibrant elements might suit a family-friendly pizza joint. Consider the transformation of Taco Bell's logo in 2016. The brand moved from a dated design to a streamlined, modern look that reflected its shift toward appealing to a more diverse and trend-focused audience. This change wasn't just cosmetic—it symbolized a broader evolution in the company's strategy and audience engagement.

Menus are another vital part of a restaurant's visual identity. They are not just lists of items but a storytelling tool that sets the tone for the dining experience. A carefully designed menu uses fonts, colors, and layout to reflect the brand's essence. A rustic, farm-to-table restaurant might use earthy tones and hand-drawn illustrations to communicate freshness and authenticity. On the other hand, a trendy café might lean on bold typography and clean lines to suggest innovation and style. Studies in menu psychology show that subtle design choices—such as placing high-margin items in prominent positions or using descriptive language—can influence customer decisions and increase sales.

Decor is where a restaurant's visual identity comes to life in its most immersive form. Every element, from lighting to table settings, should reinforce the brand's story. Consider the transformation of IHOP's new concept restaurants, which introduced modernized interiors featuring brighter colors, communal seating, and USB outlets to attract younger diners. This cohesive design doesn't just enhance the dining experience; it creates a space that resonates with the target audience, making the brand more relatable and memorable.

For restaurants looking to create visually appealing branding materials, best practices involve consistency, simplicity, and relevance. **Consistency is key** because it ensures that customers recognize your brand across every touchpoint, whether it's your website, social media, or physical signage. A unified color palette and typography set the tone, while consistent use of imagery and messaging reinforces your identity. **Simplicity matters** because overly complex designs can overwhelm and confuse customers. A clear, focused design communicates confidence and professionalism. **Relevance ensures** that every visual element aligns with your brand's values and appeals to your target audience.

The success of a restaurant's visual identity often hinges on the ability to adapt while staying true to its roots. When McDonald's rolled out its "Experience of the Future" redesign, it included sleek, modern interiors with wooden accents and digital ordering kiosks. These updates not only refreshed the brand but also aligned with changing customer expectations, bridging familiarity with innovation.

Crafting a compelling visual identity involves thoughtful design and strategic storytelling. By creating logos, menus, and decor that reflect your brand, you communicate your restaurant's values and set the stage for an unforgettable customer experience. Every choice, from the smallest detail to the overall atmosphere, contributes to how your audience perceives and connects with your restaurant.

Establishing Your Brand Voice

"If your brand doesn't stand out, you might as well not have one at all." Seth Godin's insight from *Purple Cow* challenges businesses to move beyond the ordinary and embrace the extraordinary. In a world saturated with options, establishing a distinct brand voice is not just important—it's essential. Your voice is the personality of your restaurant, expressed through tone and language. It sets the stage for emotional connections with customers, transforming a meal into a memorable experience.

Brand voice begins with clarity. What do you want your

audience to feel when they think of your restaurant? Consider a rustic bistro that prides itself on simplicity and warmth. Its voice might be calm and conversational, speaking in a tone that feels like an invitation to sit by the fire. Contrast this with a modern sushi bar catering to a young, trendy crowd. Its voice might lean on playful language and sharp wit, aligning with the vibrant energy of its target market. **A well-defined voice not only reflects your brand's identity but also creates an emotional bond that keeps customers coming back.**

Consistency is the backbone of a strong brand voice. Without it, even the most creative messages can fall flat. Imagine a farm-to-table restaurant promoting sustainability but using overly technical or corporate language in its social media posts. The disconnect between its values and tone could confuse potential customers. Instead, this brand should use accessible, heartfelt language that mirrors its mission, such as stories about local farmers or tips on reducing food waste. **When your voice is consistent across platforms, customers know exactly what to expect, building trust and loyalty over time.**

Achieving consistency requires clear guidelines. Start by defining key elements of your voice: tone, vocabulary, and style. Is your tone formal or relaxed? Do you prefer short, punchy phrases or more descriptive storytelling? Once established, apply these choices uniformly across all channels, from menus to emails to in-person interactions. Take inspiration from brands like Shake Shack, which has mastered the art of conversational messaging. Whether in their cheeky Instagram captions or customer-friendly packaging, their tone remains unmistakably theirs—inviting, approachable, and fun.

To maintain this cohesion, training your team is crucial. Your employees are the most direct representation of your brand. Their words, whether spoken at a table or written in a follow-up email, should echo your established voice. If your tone is warm and personable, ensure hosts and servers embody this approach. A cold, indifferent greeting at the door could undermine months of thoughtful branding efforts. **Regular workshops and clear reference materials can help staff internalize your voice, ensuring every customer interaction aligns with your brand's personality.**

Digital platforms provide an excellent canvas to refine and amplify your voice. Social media captions, blog posts, and website copy should all reflect the same tone and style. Consider the example of Wendy's, whose cheeky, irreverent voice on Twitter has redefined fast-food marketing. By leaning into humor and clever wordplay, the brand has captured attention and strengthened its relationship with a younger audience. While not every restaurant needs to be as bold, this approach underscores the importance of finding a tone that resonates with your unique audience.

Consistency also extends to visual elements. The way your words appear—fonts, spacing, and color schemes—should complement your voice. A fine dining restaurant, for instance, may opt for elegant typography and minimalist design, reinforcing its sophisticated tone. In contrast, a family-friendly diner might use bright colors and playful fonts that match its upbeat, casual language. **When visual and verbal elements work together, they create a unified message that strengthens brand recognition.**

Maintaining a consistent voice requires vigilance and flexibility. As your audience evolves, so should your voice. Monitor customer feedback to ensure your tone still resonates, and don't hesitate to adjust when needed. For example, a traditional steakhouse targeting older diners might start incorporating modern phrases or a lighter tone to appeal to younger guests without alienating its core audience. **Staying true to your brand while**

embracing small adaptations keeps your voice fresh and relevant.

Establishing and maintaining a strong brand voice is not just about crafting catchy phrases or clever taglines. It's about creating a cohesive identity that speaks to the heart of your audience. By aligning your tone and language with your values, training your team to embody your voice, and ensuring consistency across platforms, you turn communication into connection. This connection, built on trust and understanding, is what transforms one-time diners into lifelong advocates for your restaurant.

Aligning Your Brand with Customer Expectations

"Your brand is what other people say about you when you're not in the room." Jeff Bezos's reflection captures the essence of why aligning your brand with customer expectations is vital. A brand isn't just the story you tell—it's the reality your customers experience. The gap between these two perspectives can make or break trust, loyalty, and long-term growth. Achieving alignment requires ongoing evaluation, strategic adaptation, and a clear understanding of what your audience values most.

Conducting a brand audit is the first step in bridging any disconnect. An audit isn't just a review of logos or messaging; it's a comprehensive assessment of how your brand is perceived across all touchpoints. This process includes reviewing online reviews, customer feedback, and social media mentions to identify common themes in how customers view your brand. Pay attention to recurring words or sentiments—whether they praise your speedy service or criticize your confusing menu design. **This feedback reveals where your brand aligns with customer expectations and where it falls short.**

Evaluate every aspect of your branding, from visuals to the

tone of voice. Does your logo reflect the energy and ethos of your restaurant? Are your promotional materials consistent with your in-person dining experience? For instance, a café marketing itself as a cozy, quiet retreat shouldn't feature loud, flashy graphics or overly casual language on its website. **Your brand elements should work together to create a unified, authentic experience that matches what your customers anticipate.**

Adapting to evolving customer needs is equally critical. Customers' preferences shift over time, influenced by cultural trends, economic changes, and personal habits. Restaurants that fail to adapt risk becoming irrelevant, even if they once held a strong position in the market. Consider the rise in demand for plant-based options. Brands like Burger King have successfully adapted by introducing meatless alternatives like the Impossible Whopper, aligning their offerings with growing consumer interest in sustainability and health. **Staying attuned to these shifts requires regularly monitoring industry trends, conducting customer surveys, and staying active on social platforms where feedback often emerges first.**

Adaptation doesn't mean abandoning your core identity; it's about evolving while staying true to your values. If your restaurant prides itself on serving locally sourced ingredients, introducing new dishes inspired by global cuisine can still fit within your ethos by showcasing local twists on international flavors. **Balancing consistency with innovation allows you to meet new demands without alienating loyal customers.**

Measuring branding success is where strategy meets accountability. Success isn't measured solely by revenue; it's reflected in metrics like customer retention, social media engagement, and net promoter scores (NPS). NPS, for example, measures how likely customers are to recommend your restaurant to others, offering a clear indicator of brand loyalty. Analyze these metrics regularly, comparing them against specific goals established during your audit. **For instance, if you aimed to improve your online reputation, track the percentage of positive reviews over time and identify any patterns in customer feedback that suggest areas for further refinement.** Another important measure is customer lifetime value (CLV). This metric highlights how much revenue a customer generates over their relationship with your brand. An increase in CLV often indicates successful alignment, as satisfied customers return frequently and spend more. Brands with strong alignment often see higher CLV due to deeper emotional connections with their audience. **Tracking these metrics provides actionable insights to refine your branding efforts continuously.**

Feedback loops play a crucial role in maintaining alignment. They ensure your brand evolves in real time alongside your customers. Encourage open communication by offering multiple channels for feedback, from in-person surveys to digital comment cards. Social media platforms like Instagram and Twitter also offer valuable, unfiltered insights into customer sentiment. Responding promptly and thoughtfully to this feedback not only strengthens trust but also signals that your brand listens and values its audience.

Ultimately, aligning your brand with customer expectations requires commitment, flexibility, and a deep understanding of the relationship between perception and reality. Conducting regular audits ensures your brand stays relevant, while adapting to changes demonstrates responsiveness to customer needs. Measuring success through clear metrics transforms alignment from a vague goal into a tangible, actionable strategy. **By staying in tune with your audience and proactively refining your approach, you create a brand that not only meets but exceeds customer expectations, fostering loyalty and long-term success.**

Application of Techniques: Crafting a Cohesive and Memorable Restaurant Brand

Brand Storytelling as a Core Element: The chapter begins with the idea that every restaurant has a story, which forms the foundation of its branding. In practice, crafting this story involves identifying the unique characteristics of your restaurant —whether it's the locally sourced ingredients, the family recipes, or the commitment to sustainability. Real-world application includes creating narratives that are consistently reflected across all brand touchpoints. For instance, a farm-to-table restaurant might include information about local farmers on their menu, feature behind-the-scenes sourcing videos on social media, and train staff to share the stories with diners.

Visual Identity as a Language: Logos, menus, and décor are powerful tools in conveying your brand's personality. A minimalist logo paired with elegant typography sends a message of sophistication, while bold colors and playful fonts communicate a family-friendly or casual atmosphere. Take Taco Bell's redesign as an example: the updated logo and modern interiors reflect its target audience's preferences and broaden its appeal. In practice, restaurants can work with graphic designers or branding experts to align their visual elements with their values and mission.

Brand Voice and Tone for Emotional Connections: Establishing a brand voice ensures that all communication—from social media posts to in-person interactions—feels authentic and cohesive. A high-end steakhouse might use formal, refined language, while a casual taco shop could lean on humor and casual tone. Consistency in tone builds trust and loyalty. For instance, Wendy's success with its witty, relatable Twitter voice demonstrates how tone can resonate deeply with an audience.

Adapting to Customer Expectations: Customer preferences are dynamic, influenced by cultural, economic, and technological trends. Restaurants must stay attuned to these shifts by regularly conducting customer surveys, monitoring reviews, and analyzing industry trends. For example, the rising demand for plant-based dishes led Burger King to introduce the Impossible Whopper, meeting sustainability-focused diners where they are. Restaurants can implement these changes without losing their core identity by introducing complementary elements rather than overhauling their entire menu or concept.

Feedback Loops to Maintain Alignment: Successful brands evolve based on customer feedback. Platforms like Yelp, Google Reviews, and Instagram are treasure troves of insights into customer perception. Actively responding to reviews—both positive and negative—shows that the restaurant values its patrons. Internally, hosting regular team meetings to review customer feedback can guide updates in service, décor, or menu offerings, ensuring that the brand consistently exceeds expectations.

Action Item Checklist

Define Your Restaurant's Story:

- Identify what makes your restaurant unique: ingredients, values, or cultural roots.
- Write a short, clear narrative that explains your restaurant's purpose and vision.
- Ensure this story is reflected in all brand communications, from websites to in-person interactions.

Develop a Cohesive Visual Identity:

- Work with a designer to create a logo that aligns with your restaurant's mission.
- Choose a consistent color palette, typography, and design style for all materials.
- Update your menu layout to reflect your brand's tone and values.

Establish and Train Staff on Brand Voice:

- Define your tone: Is it formal, casual, humorous, or sophisticated?
- Create written guidelines detailing examples of brand-consistent communication.
- Conduct regular training to ensure staff embodies your brand's voice.

Adapt to Changing Customer Needs:

- Conduct biannual customer surveys to identify emerging trends.
- Use social media analytics to monitor engagement and adjust strategies.
- Test new dishes, designs, or events that align with observed preferences.

Measure Branding Success:

- Track metrics like Net Promoter Scores (NPS) and Customer Lifetime Value (CLV).
- Monitor social media engagement and online reviews for changes in sentiment.
- Regularly compare branding efforts with revenue data to assess impact.

Build Feedback Loops:

- Create multiple channels for customer input, such as surveys, comment cards, or QR codes.
- Review feedback weekly to identify actionable insights.
- Share updates based on customer feedback to demonstrate responsiveness.

Resource List

Tools:

- **Canva**: A design tool for creating logos, menus, and social media posts.
- **Hootsuite**: A social media management platform for maintaining consistent voice and tone.
- **SurveyMonkey**: For designing and distributing customer feedback surveys.

Books and Reading Material:

- **"Purple Cow" by Seth Godin**: Encourages businesses to stand out by embracing uniqueness.
- **"Start with Why" by Simon Sinek**: A guide to defining and communicating your brand's core purpose.
- **"Brand Sense" by Martin Lindstrom**: Explores how multi-sensory branding builds stronger connections.

Additional Resources:

- **Coursera: Brand Management Courses**: Online classes covering visual identity and branding strategy.
- **Yelp for Business**: A platform offering tools to engage with customer reviews and analytics.
- **National Restaurant Association**: Resources on industry trends and customer behavior.

Integrating Insights into Practice

By combining the actionable techniques outlined in this chapter with the resource tools and examples provided, restaurant owners can create a brand that not only attracts but also retains customers. The principles of clarity, consistency, and authenticity are not static; they require ongoing evaluation and adaptation to remain relevant and impactful. Through thoughtful execution of these strategies, a restaurant transforms from a dining spot to a memorable brand that resonates deeply with its audience.

CHAPTER 3

CRAFTING A WINNING MARKETING PLAN

TURN GOALS INTO ACTION WITH AN EFFECTIVE STRATEGY

What makes a restaurant stand out in a sea of options? It's not just great food or a prime location; it's a clear and focused marketing plan that turns your vision into reality. A well-designed plan serves as the blueprint for attracting customers, building loyalty, and ensuring long-term success. Without it, even the best restaurants risk fading into the background. This chapter explores how to create a strategy that aligns your goals with actionable steps, transforming your aspirations into measurable outcomes.

Every restaurant, from bustling cafes to upscale eateries, faces unique challenges when it comes to marketing. Some aim to fill tables during off-peak hours, while others want to attract a younger, tech-savvy audience. Crafting an effective plan starts with understanding what sets your restaurant apart and how to communicate that clearly to the people you want to reach. A strong strategy isn't about trying everything; it's about focusing on what works and doing it well.

Marketing isn't a one-size-fits-all solution—it's a dynamic process that adapts to changing trends, customer needs, and new tools. A plan rooted in thoughtful research and clear objectives makes it easier to adjust as you grow. For example, a social media campaign promoting a seasonal menu can drive traffic in the short term, while a loyalty program keeps regulars engaged over time. Each step in the plan should connect back to your overarching goals, creating a system that's as cohesive as it is flexible.

One of the most important aspects of a successful marketing plan is understanding your audience. Knowing their preferences, habits, and values allows you to speak directly to their needs. For instance, families looking for convenience and affordability will respond to messages that highlight value and kid-friendly options. Meanwhile, foodies seeking unique dining experiences might be drawn in by behind-the-scenes content or chef collaborations. By tailoring your efforts to your audience, you can build meaningful connections that go beyond the plate.

Another key element is consistency. From the colors on your website to the tone of your social media posts, every touchpoint should reflect the same brand personality. This not only reinforces your identity but also builds trust with your audience. Whether someone discovers your restaurant through a glowing review or an eye-catching ad, their experience should match the expectations you've set.

A well-executed marketing plan also requires collaboration. It's not just the responsibility of one person or department; it's a collective effort that involves everyone, from the kitchen staff to the servers. When your team understands the goals and their role in achieving them, they become ambassadors for your brand. Whether it's a barista chatting about a new promotion or a manager responding to online reviews, every interaction contributes to the bigger picture.

Crafting a winning marketing plan isn't just about bringing in more customers—it's about creating an experience that keeps them coming back. This chapter breaks down the process into clear, actionable steps, giving you the tools to turn ideas into results. By the end, you'll have the framework needed to not only meet your goals but exceed them.

Why You Need a Marketing Plan

Imagine a small neighborhood café, bustling with customers during its opening month. The energy is high, the tables are full, and word of mouth is strong. Then, a few weeks later, things begin to slow down. The café's owners, unsure how to sustain the initial buzz, try random promotions and post sporadically on social media, hoping something will stick. As the weeks go by, the crowd thins, and the once-busy café struggles to maintain visibility. This scenario is all too common in the restaurant industry, where many establishments operate without a clear marketing plan, relying on guesswork instead of strategy.

A structured marketing plan offers more than just a list of promotional ideas. It provides a **roadmap for consistent growth**, ensuring that every effort aligns with your long-term goals. Without this framework, even the most innovative campaigns can falter, leading to wasted resources and missed opportunities. A well-crafted plan enables you to allocate time and money effectively, ensuring that your efforts have the maximum impact on customer engagement and revenue.

One of the most significant benefits of a structured approach is its ability to create **clarity and focus**. When you know exactly what you want to achieve—whether it's driving more foot traffic on slow nights or increasing repeat visits—you can tailor your efforts to meet those objectives. For instance, if your goal is to attract a younger audience, your strategy might emphasize social media platforms like Instagram or TikTok, showcasing visually striking dishes or behind-the-scenes videos of your chef at work. This targeted approach ensures that every tactic serves a purpose, reducing the risk of spreading resources too thin.

Operating without a plan often leads to **disjointed efforts and inconsistent messaging**. A restaurant that posts haphazardly on social media or runs uncoordinated promotions risks confusing its audience. Consistency is critical in building trust and loyalty; customers should recognize your brand instantly, whether they see your ad online or walk into your dining room. A marketing plan ensures that all your touchpoints—emails, social posts, in-store signage—convey the same personality, tone, and values.

Planning also helps mitigate common challenges, such as responding to slow periods or adapting to market changes. Seasonal dips in traffic, for example, are a reality for many restaurants, but a proactive marketing plan can turn these lulls into opportunities. Consider introducing seasonal menus, themed promotions, or exclusive discounts during quieter months. By planning ahead, you not only address challenges but also strengthen your relationship with customers, giving them reasons to return when they might otherwise stay home.

An effective marketing plan is built on **key elements that work together seamlessly**. At its core, the plan starts with defining your goals. Are you looking to boost lunch sales by 20% or attract more catering clients? Clear, measurable objectives act as your north star, guiding every decision you make. From there, identifying your target audience becomes essential. Understanding their preferences, habits, and needs allows you to tailor your efforts, making your messaging feel personal and relevant. A family-friendly diner might emphasize kid-friendly meals and community events, while a high-end steakhouse could highlight its exclusive wine pairings and sophisticated atmosphere.

Another cornerstone of your plan is a detailed strategy for implementation. This includes setting a timeline for campaigns, assigning roles within your team, and choosing the tools and platforms that will amplify your message. Whether it's running geo-targeted ads or hosting local events, every tactic should align with your overall objectives, creating a cohesive and compelling story.

Finally, tracking and measuring results is essential to refining your efforts. Metrics such as customer retention rates, social media engagement, and revenue growth provide valuable insights into what's working and what needs adjustment. A successful marketing plan isn't static; it evolves based on performance and feedback, allowing you to stay ahead of trends and meet your customers' changing expectations.

A restaurant without a marketing plan is like a ship without a compass—drifting without direction, at the mercy of unpredictable currents. By embracing structure and strategy, you not only navigate challenges but also chart a clear course toward sustained success. Through thoughtful planning and execution, you can ensure that every effort contributes to a stronger, more recognizable brand that resonates with customers and keeps them coming back.

Mapping Out Your Marketing Strategy

Why do some marketing strategies seem to effortlessly capture attention while others barely make a ripple? The answer often lies not in the quality of the offering but in the alignment of the marketing strategy with the goals and audience of the business. For restaurants, where competition is fierce and customer expectations constantly evolve, having a mapped-out strategy is not a luxury—it's a necessity.

Choosing the right channels to promote your restaurant begins with a clear understanding of your goals. A family-friendly diner looking to attract local patrons may prioritize platforms like Facebook or community bulletin boards, while a trendy urban café aiming to reach a younger, digitally savvy crowd might focus on Instagram and TikTok. Each platform has its own strengths and audience demographics, which must align with your marketing objectives. This targeted approach ensures your efforts resonate with the right people and drive measurable results.

Digital strategies play a critical role in modern marketing plans, as highlighted in "Don't 86 Your Restaurant Sales." The book emphasizes that ignoring online opportunities in today's market is like leaving money on the table. Consider integrating Google My Business to improve your visibility in local searches or utilizing email marketing to build lasting relationships with customers. Online tools allow for precision targeting, meaning you can reach diners based on their location, dining preferences, and even previous engagement with your brand.

Planning effective promotions and campaigns is another cornerstone of a successful marketing strategy. A promotion should never be a one-off event without context; it should fit within a larger narrative that reflects your brand's identity. For example, a steakhouse might create a "Summer Grill Nights" campaign, offering seasonal specials and sharing grilling tips on social media. This not only attracts customers but also positions the restaurant as an expert in its niche. Seasonal campaigns, loyalty programs, and collaborations with local influencers are all strategies that, when planned thoughtfully, yield significant returns.

Timing is everything when it comes to campaigns. A cohesive marketing calendar helps ensure your efforts are consistent and well-coordinated. This calendar should outline key dates, such as holidays, local events, or your restaurant's anniversary, around which you can build promotions. Planning in advance allows you to create integrated campaigns that include social media posts, email newsletters, and in-store signage, all working together to amplify your message.

Tools like Trello, Google Calendar, or specialized software such as Hootsuite can simplify the process of organizing your marketing efforts. These platforms allow you to schedule posts, track campaign progress, and ensure all team members are on the same page. The advantage of using these tools is not just in efficiency but in the ability to maintain consistency across multiple channels. A mismatched tone or aesthetic between platforms can dilute your message, while seamless integration reinforces your brand's identity.

Successful marketing strategies also require ongoing evaluation and adaptation. Tracking performance metrics, such as social media engagement, reservation increases, or coupon redemptions, provides insights into what resonates with your audience. If a campaign underperforms, consider tweaking the messaging, adjusting the timing, or exploring a different channel. Marketing is as much about experimentation as it is about planning, and the willingness to adapt is what separates thriving businesses from those that stagnate.

Mapping out your marketing strategy transforms abstract goals into actionable steps. By choosing the right channels, planning meaningful promotions, and utilizing tools to maintain a cohesive calendar, you create a framework for success. This approach not only ensures your restaurant stays relevant in a crowded market but also positions you as a brand that understands and meets the needs of its customers.

Budgeting for Marketing Success

"Marketing without a budget is like dining without a menu— you might stumble upon something satisfying, but chances are you'll waste time and resources before finding what works." This insight from *Restaurant Success by the Numbers* underscores the importance of strategic financial planning when it comes to promoting your business. A well-allocated marketing budget not only maximizes your reach but ensures that every dollar spent brings measurable value to your brand.

Effective allocation begins with understanding your restaurant's revenue and profit margins. Industry experts recommend dedicating between 3% and 10% of your gross revenue to marketing efforts, depending on the size of your establishment and the competitive landscape. For instance, a small neighborhood café with a loyal customer base may focus on the lower end of this range, while a new fine dining restaurant might need to invest more heavily to build awareness. Regardless of the percentage, it's crucial to balance ambition with sustainability— overspending in the short term can harm long-term profitability.

Prioritizing strategies with a high return on investment is the cornerstone of an effective marketing budget. Digital platforms such as Google Ads and social media marketing often deliver significant results at relatively low costs. For example, a targeted Facebook ad campaign costing as little as $500 can generate thousands of impressions among local diners, driving foot traffic and reservations. Meanwhile, maintaining an active and engaging Instagram profile offers a nearly free way to showcase your menu and ambiance, leveraging user-generated content to amplify your message.

Print and traditional media may still have a place in your plan, but they require careful consideration. Flyers, local newspaper ads, and sponsorships can be valuable for certain audiences, such as older patrons or local communities. However, these methods often come with higher costs and less precise tracking. Weighing their effectiveness against digital alternatives is essential to ensure they align with your goals.

Budgeting also involves planning for seasonal fluctuations and special campaigns. High-traffic periods, such as holidays or local festivals, offer prime opportunities to increase visibility. For instance, allocating funds toward a Valentine's Day prix fixe menu promotion or a summer patio series can create buzz and drive incremental revenue. These campaigns should be mapped out in advance within a cohesive marketing calendar, ensuring that resources are distributed evenly across the year without overspending in one quarter.

Flexibility is another critical aspect of successful budgeting. Marketing strategies often involve experimentation, and not every campaign will yield the desired results. Setting aside a contingency fund—typically 10% of your total marketing budget —allows you to pivot quickly when new opportunities arise or adjustments are needed. For example, if a last-minute food festival sponsorship becomes available, having reserved funds can enable participation without derailing other initiatives.

Real-world examples highlight the power of thoughtful budgeting. A mid-sized pizzeria in Chicago used a $1,000 monthly marketing budget to dominate its local market by focusing on social media ads and a rewards program. By investing $700 in targeted Instagram ads showcasing their signature deep-dish pizza and using the remaining $300 to promote a customer loyalty app, they increased repeat business by 15% in six months. This dual strategy demonstrated the impact of aligning budget allocations with specific goals: building brand awareness and fostering customer retention.

Low-cost, high-impact strategies are invaluable for businesses with tight budgets. Collaborating with local influencers can yield significant visibility for the cost of a free meal, while hosting community events like cooking classes or trivia nights can attract customers and generate buzz. Partnerships with nearby businesses, such as cross-promotions with a local brewery, can expand your reach at minimal expense. These tactics emphasize creativity over cost, proving that impactful marketing doesn't always require a hefty investment.

Budget-friendly marketing plans also benefit from leveraging free tools and resources. Platforms like Canva offer easy design solutions for creating professional-looking promotional materials, while Google My Business ensures your restaurant appears in local search results at no cost. Email marketing platforms such as Mailchimp allow you to communicate directly with your audience for a fraction of the cost of traditional mail campaigns, offering analytics to track engagement and refine your approach.

The key to successful marketing budgeting lies in strategic allocation, prioritizing high-ROI strategies, and embracing flexibility. By combining thoughtful planning with a willingness to adapt, your restaurant can achieve sustained growth while maintaining financial health. Whether your budget is $500 or $50,000, the right approach ensures every dollar spent strengthens your brand and resonates with your audience.

Executing Your Plan and Monitoring Progress

"Plans are worthless, but planning is everything." Dwight Eisenhower's words resonate deeply in the realm of marketing. While even the best-laid strategies require adjustments, having a thoughtful framework ensures you're prepared to execute effectively, measure outcomes, and adapt as needed. For restaurants, the ability to implement campaigns seamlessly and pivot quickly is the difference between a fleeting buzz and sustained success.

Seamless execution begins with clarity. Each campaign should have a specific objective, whether it's increasing weekday reservations, promoting a new dish, or driving repeat visits through loyalty programs. Clearly defined goals streamline implementation by aligning all efforts under a common purpose. For example, a promotion targeting happy hour traffic should integrate messaging across social media, in-store signage, and email newsletters, ensuring consistency and clarity at every customer touchpoint.

A cohesive timeline is the backbone of seamless campaign execution. Marketing calendars help map out promotions, seasonal campaigns, and key dates, reducing the risk of overlap or resource strain. For instance, tools like Google Calendar or Trello allow teams to plan months in advance, assigning tasks, deadlines, and responsibilities to keep projects on track. An organized schedule not only improves coordination but also provides a clear visual of how campaigns align with larger business objectives.

Tracking performance is equally critical. Without data, it's impossible to determine whether efforts are meeting expectations or require recalibration. Tools like Google Analytics, Facebook Insights, and point-of-sale software provide actionable insights into customer behavior, campaign engagement, and revenue impact. For example, a restaurant promoting its Sunday brunch might monitor Instagram engagement metrics such as likes and shares while comparing these trends against reservation bookings. These data points reveal whether the campaign resonates with the target audience or needs refinement.

Monitoring performance also involves setting benchmarks and key performance indicators (KPIs). Metrics like customer acquisition cost (CAC), return on ad spend (ROAS), and click-through rates (CTR) offer quantitative measures of success. However, qualitative feedback, such as customer comments or staff observations, can provide valuable context that numbers alone might miss. For instance, if a discount campaign drives traffic but generates complaints about service delays, operational adjustments may be necessary to sustain long-term benefits.

Adaptability ensures that campaigns remain effective in the face of unexpected challenges or underwhelming results. When marketing efforts fall short, swift pivots prevent wasted resources and lost opportunities. A restaurant launching a new menu might notice lower-than-expected customer interest during the first week. By analyzing feedback and performance data, the team could refine their approach, perhaps emphasizing specific dishes through high-quality photos or leveraging influencer partnerships to create buzz.

Adaptation doesn't mean abandoning your strategy; it's about learning and iterating. Establishing feedback loops creates a system for continuous improvement. Regular post-campaign reviews help identify strengths, weaknesses, and actionable takeaways for future efforts. For example, if a paid social media ad performed well among one demographic but missed another, adjustments can fine-tune targeting in subsequent campaigns. This iterative process not only enhances effectiveness but fosters a culture of innovation within your marketing team.

Real-time monitoring tools further enhance adaptability. Platforms like Hootsuite allow marketers to track campaign performance across social channels, providing early warnings if engagement metrics fall below expectations. These tools enable immediate course corrections, such as modifying ad copy, adjusting audience targeting, or reallocating budgets toward higher-performing channels. A restaurant using email marketing might identify low open rates mid-campaign and revise its subject lines to spark curiosity and re-engage recipients.

Examples of successful pivots illustrate the power of flexibility. During the early days of the pandemic, many restaurants faced significant declines in dine-in traffic. Quick-thinking businesses that shifted focus to delivery and takeout promotions often outperformed competitors. One pizzeria used geotargeted social media ads to promote curbside pickup, achieving a 20% increase in sales during a period when many others struggled to break even. This shift highlights how agility, supported by data and customer insights, can transform challenges into opportunities. Sustained success in marketing relies on balancing thoughtful planning with agile execution. By combining clear objectives, effective tools, and performance tracking, restaurants can execute campaigns that not only meet goals but exceed customer expectations. When challenges arise, adaptability ensures that every campaign remains aligned with evolving needs, creating a resilient and impactful marketing strategy.

Application of Techniques: Crafting a Winning Marketing Plan for Restaurants

This chapter provides an in-depth framework for restaurant owners to design, execute, and refine marketing strategies effectively. Below is a detailed exploration of the key techniques and processes covered, alongside real-world applications:

Defining Clear Goals: Every successful marketing plan starts with specific, measurable objectives. Goals provide direction, helping restaurant owners align their strategies with their overall business vision. For instance, if the aim is to increase weekday lunch sales by 15%, the strategy could involve launching a targeted lunch special campaign on social media. By identifying a clear objective, restaurants can focus their efforts and avoid wasting resources on initiatives that don't contribute to their goals.

Understanding the Audience: A deep understanding of the target demographic is critical to tailoring effective messaging. Restaurants must consider factors like dining habits, spending patterns, and preferences. For example, a family-oriented restaurant might emphasize value-packed meals, kid-friendly amenities, and flexible dining hours. Conversely, a fine-dining establishment might focus on exclusivity, featuring chef-led events or premium wine pairings to appeal to affluent diners seeking unique experiences.

Choosing the Right Channels: The chapter emphasizes the importance of selecting communication platforms that align with audience preferences. A trendy café catering to millennials and Gen Z might focus on Instagram and TikTok for their highly visual appeal, while a neighborhood diner targeting local families could prioritize Facebook and email newsletters. This targeted approach ensures that marketing efforts resonate with the audience and generate meaningful engagement.

Crafting Consistent Branding: Consistency across all touchpoints is essential for building trust and recognition. From the design of the menu to the tone of social media posts, every element should reinforce the restaurant's identity. For example, a casual burger joint might use playful language and bold colors, while a high-end sushi bar would favor minimalist design and sophisticated messaging. This consistency ensures that customers have a seamless experience across digital and physical interactions.

Building a Marketing Calendar: A well-structured marketing calendar helps restaurants coordinate campaigns, promotions, and content creation. For example, a restaurant might plan seasonal events, such as a summer patio series or holiday-themed menus, and map out corresponding social media posts, email campaigns, and in-store promotions. Tools like Trello or Google Calendar can simplify planning and ensure all team members stay informed.

Tracking Performance Metrics: To gauge success, restaurants must track KPIs such as customer acquisition cost (CAC), return on ad spend (ROAS), and customer retention rates. For instance, a restaurant running a coupon campaign might track how many customers redeem the offer and how often they return. Insights from these metrics allow for data-driven decisions, ensuring future campaigns are even more effective.

Embracing Adaptability: Marketing is an iterative process, and plans must evolve based on performance and feedback. If a campaign underperforms, restaurants should analyze the data to identify gaps and pivot accordingly. For example, a poorly performing social media ad might require adjustments to its imagery, copy, or audience targeting.

Action Item Checklist

Define Clear Goals:

- Identify short-term and long-term objectives.
- Ensure goals are specific, measurable, and time-bound (e.g., increase monthly reservations by 10%).

Research Your Target Audience:

- Gather data on customer demographics, preferences, and dining habits through surveys, reviews, and feedback.
- Create detailed customer personas to guide messaging.

Choose Effective Marketing Channels:

- Assess the platforms your target audience uses most.
- Allocate resources to channels that align with your goals (e.g., Instagram for visual promotions, email for loyalty programs).

Develop a Marketing Calendar:

- Outline key dates, such as holidays, local events, or seasonal menu launches.
- Assign roles and deadlines for content creation, promotions, and campaign execution.

Ensure Brand Consistency:

- Audit all touchpoints, including website design, menu layout, and social media profiles, to ensure they reflect your brand identity.
- Standardize messaging across all channels for a cohesive experience.

Track and Analyze Performance:

- Use tools like Google Analytics, Facebook Insights, and point-of-sale software to monitor engagement, revenue impact, and customer feedback.
- Regularly review campaign results to identify strengths and areas for improvement.

Adapt and Refine Strategies:

- Conduct post-campaign reviews to gather insights.
- Adjust messaging, targeting, or budget allocation based on data and feedback.

Resource List

Tools:

- **Google Analytics**: Tracks website traffic, customer demographics, and campaign performance.

- **Hootsuite:** Schedules social media posts and monitors engagement metrics.
- **Trello:** Organizes marketing calendars and assigns team responsibilities.
- **Mailchimp:** Simplifies email marketing with automated campaigns and analytics.

Books and Reading Material:

- *Restaurant Success by the Numbers* by Roger Fields: Offers financial planning insights for effective budgeting.
- *Don't 86 Your Restaurant Sales*: Explores the role of digital marketing in driving restaurant growth.

Additional Resources:

- Online courses on marketing fundamentals (e.g., Coursera's Digital Marketing Specialization).
- Industry forums and communities like RestaurantOwner.com for peer advice and resources.
- Local business development organizations that offer workshops and networking opportunities.

CHAPTER 4
OPTIMIZING YOUR MENU FOR MARKETING SUCCESS

HOW A STRATEGIC MENU DESIGN BOOSTS SALES AND ATTRACTS CUSTOMERS

A menu is more than a list of dishes; it's a stage where every item competes for attention, enticing diners and guiding their choices. Restaurants often underestimate the power of their menu to influence spending habits, but strategic design can transform it into a tool that drives revenue and elevates the customer experience. From the placement of high-margin items to the descriptions that stir cravings, every detail plays a role in shaping how diners interact with your offerings.

Imagine walking into a bustling bistro, scanning a menu, and immediately spotting a chef's special that seems irresistible. This is no coincidence—it's the result of thoughtful planning and design. A well-optimized menu doesn't just showcase what's available; it subtly steers customers toward the dishes you most want to sell. When done right, it blends psychology and marketing to enhance satisfaction while improving your bottom line.

For many restaurants, the menu is often overlooked as a static tool rather than a dynamic asset. Yet, menus can be tailored to reflect changing seasons, highlight signature dishes, and support broader marketing campaigns. Featuring a seasonal dessert during the holidays, for example, creates excitement and urgency while reinforcing your restaurant's connection to the occasion. By aligning the menu with your overall goals, you ensure it remains fresh and engaging.

At its core, menu optimization is about balance—showcasing variety without overwhelming, focusing on profitability while preserving choice. Each menu item should serve a purpose, whether it's a high-margin appetizer designed to boost check averages or a carefully crafted entree that anchors your restaurant's identity. Even the smallest tweaks, like grouping items into logical categories or adding visual cues, can have a measurable impact on how diners order.

This chapter explores the ways your menu can become one of your most valuable marketing tools. From design principles that catch the eye to strategies for promoting high-margin dishes, you'll uncover how a thoughtful approach to your menu can achieve more than you might expect. It's about creating a seamless experience where every decision, from the font size to the layout, works together to showcase your restaurant at its best.

Understanding the Role of the Menu in Marketing

A guest once entered a well-known bistro and scanned the menu, only to leave a few minutes later, saying it "didn't feel right." The food, atmosphere, and location were top-notch, but the menu failed to communicate any of it. This simple moment reveals a truth many restaurants overlook: menus are more than informational; they're influential. The menu serves as a silent salesperson, shaping perceptions, guiding choices, and driving sales.

Menus hold power because they connect directly to customer

decisions. Studies have shown that the way items are presented —through placement, descriptions, and pricing—can impact what diners order and how much they spend. For instance, anchoring high-priced items near mid-tier options subtly pushes customers toward dishes that feel like better value. This isn't manipulation; it's psychology. A strategically designed menu creates a balance, ensuring customers feel both guided and in control of their choices.

A strong menu doesn't overwhelm; it inspires curiosity and builds trust. Restaurants that succeed in using their menu as a marketing tool often focus on clarity, visual appeal, and emotional connection. Consider a family-focused diner that includes a "Kid's Favorites" section with fun graphics and comforting descriptions like "Grandma's Mac & Cheese." This approach highlights value, creates a welcoming feel, and speaks directly to the audience's priorities. Similarly, a fine dining restaurant might use elegant fonts and rich descriptions like "Seared Atlantic Salmon with Citrus Beurre Blanc" to reflect its upscale identity.

One critical aspect of successful menus is storytelling. A thoughtfully crafted description can elevate an item from ordinary to irresistible. For example, a café offering an "Autumn Harvest Salad" might highlight its local ingredients and seasonal appeal, creating an emotional connection with customers. Words like "handpicked" and "locally sourced" suggest care and quality, reinforcing the restaurant's values and drawing in diners who prioritize fresh, sustainable food.

Another strategy is leveraging menu layout. Placing high-margin items in prominent positions—like the top-right corner of a two-panel menu—draws attention to the dishes that benefit the business most. Restaurants that frame these items with visual cues, such as a subtle box or highlighted background, see measurable increases in orders. Effective layouts combine these techniques with logical categories that guide diners naturally, ensuring every option feels accessible and appealing.

The role of pricing is equally significant. Guests rarely choose items based solely on cost, but the way prices are presented can influence perceived value. Removing currency symbols, for instance, makes diners less likely to fixate on price and more likely to focus on the dish itself. Research also suggests that prices ending in .95 or .99 feel less upscale, while round numbers create a sense of simplicity and quality. A well-designed menu uses pricing as a tool to enhance the dining experience rather than as a distraction.

Understanding the menu's role in marketing goes beyond design—it requires regular evaluation and adaptation. Successful restaurants treat their menus as living documents, updating them to reflect seasonal changes, customer feedback, and business goals. A seafood restaurant, for example, might rotate its menu quarterly, introducing fresh catches to keep regulars excited while showcasing the chef's versatility. This not only keeps offerings relevant but also provides opportunities to market new dishes through social media and in-house promotions.

A restaurant's menu is more than a list of options; it's a reflection of its identity and values. When thoughtfully designed, it can turn casual diners into loyal customers, influence spending habits, and reinforce brand perception. By treating the menu as a core element of marketing, restaurants can maximize its impact, ensuring it communicates the experience they promise to deliver.

Designing a Customer-Friendly Menu

Have you ever wondered why some menus make you excited to order while others feel like a confusing maze? The answer often lies in design. A well-thought-out menu layout can transform the way customers experience a restaurant, influencing their choices and creating a sense of ease and excitement. On the other hand, poor design can frustrate diners, slow down decisions, and even impact how much they spend. A menu isn't just a list of options—it's a visual and psychological tool that shapes the dining experience from the moment it's handed over.

Clarity is the cornerstone of an effective menu. When customers can quickly scan the layout and understand the offerings, they're more likely to feel confident and satisfied with their choices. The most successful menus use strategic spacing, logical categories, and minimal distractions to create a seamless reading experience. For example, grouping similar items under clear headings like "Appetizers" or "Seafood Specialties" makes it easy for diners to focus on what interests them. Clean lines and consistent font styles also play a crucial role, ensuring the menu looks polished and professional.

Highlighting high-margin items is another essential practice in menu design. Restaurants often use visual techniques like boxes, bold text, or subtle colors to draw attention to their most profitable dishes. Research in "The Restaurant Manager's Handbook" reveals that diners' eyes tend to be drawn to specific "hot zones" on a menu, such as the top-right corner. Placing signature or high-profit dishes in these areas increases the likelihood they'll be ordered, boosting overall revenue without adding pressure to the customer. For instance, a steakhouse might feature its premium ribeye in a standout box with a mouthwatering description, encouraging customers to see it as a must-try option.

Effective design isn't about overwhelming the customer with choices—it's about guiding them. Overly cluttered menus with too many items can lead to decision fatigue, causing diners to pick safe, lower-priced options or feel rushed. A streamlined menu with a manageable number of options not only enhances the dining experience but also allows the kitchen to focus on quality and consistency. Successful restaurants often revise their menus regularly, removing underperforming items to make space for seasonal dishes or new creations that align with their brand and profitability goals.

Avoiding common design mistakes is just as important as implementing best practices. One frequent misstep is using overly elaborate fonts or tiny text that's difficult to read, especially in dim lighting. Similarly, including prices in a column can encourage customers to focus on cost instead of the dish descriptions, which can lead to fewer high-margin orders. Removing currency symbols and aligning prices subtly next to the descriptions shifts the focus back to the food and its value. Another pitfall is inconsistent branding. A menu that doesn't match the restaurant's identity—whether it's a casual café or an upscale dining room—can create a disconnect, leaving customers confused about what to expect.

Design also extends to visuals, such as photos or illustrations. While a single, high-quality image can enhance the appeal of a dish, overloading the menu with pictures can cheapen its overall feel. Restaurants that rely on elegant design elements, such as tasteful borders or small icons, strike a balance between visual interest and professionalism. For example, a family-friendly diner might include a small graphic of a sun next to its breakfast specials, adding charm without distracting from the main content.

Crafting a customer-friendly menu requires more than creativity—it's a process rooted in strategy and psychology. By focusing on layout, highlighting key items, and avoiding common errors, restaurants can design menus that are both appealing and functional. A well-executed menu doesn't just inform; it inspires confidence, enhances the dining experience, and ultimately drives success.

Writing Enticing Menu Descriptions

"Food tastes better when you have a story to tell." This sentiment, often shared among culinary professionals, underscores the importance of menu descriptions. The words used to describe a dish are not just placeholders; they are the gateway to a customer's first impression, setting the tone for their dining experience. A well-crafted description does more than list ingredients—it paints a picture, awakens the senses, and aligns with the brand's personality. The right words can elevate a simple dish into a must-try experience, while poor descriptions can leave even the most exquisite creations overlooked.

Using sensory language is one of the most effective ways to make menu descriptions enticing. Words that evoke taste, texture, and aroma create a vivid mental image of the dish, compelling customers to imagine it before they've even ordered. For example, describing a dessert as a "silky chocolate mousse with a hint of rich espresso" transports the reader into the indulgent experience of eating it. Research shows that diners are more likely to order dishes when the descriptions engage their senses, tapping into emotions rather than just logic. It's not enough to state what's on the plate—successful descriptions make the diner feel what it will be like to enjoy it.

Conciseness is equally important. Long, verbose descriptions risk overwhelming the reader or delaying decision-making, which can frustrate both the customer and the staff. A great description balances sensory appeal with brevity, focusing on the key elements that make the dish unique. For instance, "Tender grilled salmon glazed with a tangy citrus sauce" is more impactful than a lengthy list of ingredients or preparation methods. Every word should serve a purpose, guiding the diner's choice while leaving just enough mystery to spark curiosity.

Incorporating the brand's voice into menu text ties the dining experience back to the restaurant's identity. A casual café might lean on playful, lighthearted language, such as "Our classic burger, piled high with all the good stuff!" Conversely, a fine dining establishment may opt for elegant, refined descriptions like "Herb-crusted lamb, paired with a velvety rosemary jus." The tone of the menu should mirror the atmosphere of the restaurant, ensuring that customers know what to expect from their experience. Consistency in language reinforces the brand, making it more memorable and trustworthy.

Common pitfalls in menu writing often stem from a lack of focus or an overreliance on generic terms. Words like "delicious" or "tasty," while positive, lack the specificity needed to create an emotional connection. Similarly, failing to highlight what makes a dish special—its freshness, preparation style, or cultural roots —can cause it to fade into the background. An effective description doesn't just inform; it persuades, turning curiosity into anticipation.

Examples of successful menu strategies highlight the power of description. A bistro that renamed its "chicken and rice" to "Savory roasted chicken over fragrant jasmine rice with a side of tangy pickled vegetables" saw a noticeable increase in orders for the dish. This transformation wasn't about changing the recipe; it was about changing the perception. By emphasizing aroma and complementary flavors, the dish stood out as a thoughtfully crafted offering rather than a basic option. Stories about ingredients or preparation methods—like mentioning that the pasta is handmade daily or the vegetables are sourced from a local farm —add layers of authenticity, deepening the customer's connection to the meal.

Writing enticing menu descriptions is both an art and a

science. It requires a deep understanding of the target audience, a strong alignment with the brand's voice, and the ability to balance sensory appeal with clarity. Each word contributes to the customer's first taste of the restaurant, long before the food arrives at their table. By mastering the craft of menu descriptions, restaurants can turn a simple list of dishes into a powerful marketing tool that delights and inspires diners.

Leveraging Seasonal and Specialty Menus

"People crave what they can't have." This simple truth lies at the heart of why seasonal and specialty menus are so effective. Limited-time offerings do more than provide fresh dining options; they create a sense of urgency that encourages customers to act now rather than wait. When diners see a seasonal dish on the menu, they are not just ordering food— they're seizing an opportunity that might not come again soon. This psychological pull, known as the scarcity principle, has been studied extensively, with researchers finding that limited availability can significantly increase demand.

Seasonal menus bring a host of benefits that extend beyond attracting customers. They allow restaurants to incorporate fresh, local ingredients, which can lower costs and improve quality. Highlighting these aspects on the menu not only adds appeal but also positions the restaurant as mindful and in tune with its surroundings. For example, a farm-to-table restaurant showcasing a summer harvest salad with freshly picked heirloom tomatoes and sweet corn demonstrates its commitment to sustainability and quality. This connection between seasonality and authenticity resonates with diners, fostering trust and loyalty.

Specialty menus, on the other hand, capitalize on trends or unique dining experiences to draw in customers. Whether it's a limited-edition holiday cocktail menu or a chef's tasting series, these offerings create buzz and differentiate a restaurant from its competitors. Specialty items give customers a reason to return, especially when they feel part of something exclusive. For example, a restaurant hosting an Oktoberfest-inspired beer and bratwurst pairing menu taps into cultural excitement while driving incremental revenue during a specific window of time.

Creating urgency is key to the success of seasonal and specialty offerings. Customers are more likely to make quick decisions when they know an item won't last. Phrases like "only available for a short time" or "while supplies last" communicate this scarcity effectively, driving orders. Studies in consumer behavior show that time-limited promotions increase conversion rates, as customers fear missing out on an experience others might enjoy.

Marketing campaigns play a pivotal role in promoting seasonal and specialty menus. Social media is particularly effective, offering an instant way to share visually engaging content. High-quality photos of a limited-time dish paired with strategic captions—such as "Experience the flavors of fall with our pumpkin ravioli, available this month only"—can spark interest and encourage bookings. Email marketing also works well, especially when targeted to regular customers who value staying informed about new offerings. Loyalty program members, for instance, might receive early access to a specialty menu, further enhancing their connection to the brand.

Local collaborations amplify the reach of these campaigns. Partnering with nearby farms, breweries, or wineries to source ingredients or pair beverages aligns the restaurant with other trusted names in the community. Mentioning these partnerships in promotional materials adds credibility and reinforces the message that the menu is rooted in genuine quality. A restaurant collaborating with a popular local bakery for a Valentine's Day dessert menu not only attracts diners but also deepens ties within the community, creating a win-win for all parties involved.

While seasonal and specialty menus can be profitable, careful planning is essential to avoid pitfalls. Operational challenges, such as sourcing specific ingredients or training staff on new offerings, must be addressed ahead of time to ensure smooth execution. Tracking sales performance and customer feedback allows restaurants to refine their approach for future campaigns. For instance, if a seasonal dish receives high praise but struggles to sell, it might need better placement on the menu or more prominent marketing.

The impact of well-executed seasonal and specialty menus extends beyond immediate sales. These offerings keep the dining experience fresh, encouraging repeat visits and word-of-mouth recommendations. Diners remember unique experiences, and a menu that evolves with the seasons or introduces exciting, short-lived items remains dynamic and relevant. By balancing creativity with strategic promotion, restaurants can leverage these menus to sustain interest, build loyalty, and maximize revenue throughout the year.

Application of Techniques: Optimizing Your Menu for Marketing Success

Menus as Influential Tools: Menus are more than functional documents; they are subtle yet powerful tools that influence customer behavior. The chapter highlights that using psychology, such as anchoring high-priced items near mid-tier options, guides diners to perceive certain dishes as better value. For instance, placing a premium steak priced at $40 next to a $25 entrée encourages customers to view the $25 dish as both economical and indulgent. Restaurants can further draw attention to high-margin items by using visual cues like boxes, bold fonts, or highlighted sections. Applying these strategies ensures menus serve as sales drivers without overwhelming diners.

Storytelling Through Menu Descriptions: Sensory language transforms simple descriptions into vivid narratives. For example, replacing "grilled chicken salad" with "Tender, flame-kissed chicken atop a bed of crisp, farm-fresh greens" not only sounds appealing but also communicates quality and care. To keep descriptions concise yet compelling, focus on taste, texture, and preparation while aligning with the restaurant's brand voice. A casual café might describe a dessert as "gooey, chocolate-packed brownies," while a fine-dining restaurant could opt for "decadent, hand-crafted Valrhona chocolate squares." This precision fosters emotional connections and reflects the dining experience promised.

Highlighting Seasonal and Specialty Menus: Seasonal offerings keep menus dynamic and exciting, aligning the restaurant with local produce and culinary trends. Including phrases like "locally sourced" or "freshly harvested" reinforces authenticity and sustainability. Specialty menus, such as holiday-themed dishes or limited-time events, tap into the scarcity principle to boost sales. Promoting these offerings through social media, email campaigns, and in-house signage ensures customers are aware of their ephemeral nature. For example, a summer menu featuring "Heirloom Tomato Bruschetta with Basil Pesto" can be marketed as a must-try before the season ends.

The Role of Layout and Visual Design: Strategic layout positions high-margin dishes in prime visual hotspots, such as the top-right corner of a two-page menu. Logical categorization (e.g., appetizers, mains, desserts) enhances clarity, helping diners make quicker, more confident decisions. Avoiding clutter and ensuring consistent branding ensures the menu aligns with the restaurant's identity. For instance, a high-end steakhouse might use elegant typography and minimalistic design, while a family diner could include playful graphics and brighter colors.

Psychological Pricing Strategies: Subtle pricing techniques, such as removing currency symbols or using rounded numbers, help diners focus on the value of the dish rather than its cost. A $29 entrée without a visible dollar sign feels less expensive than one marked $29.99. This approach aligns with research indicating that simpler pricing enhances perceived value, especially in upscale settings.

Regular Evaluation and Updates: Treating the menu as a living document ensures it stays relevant and profitable. Restaurants can evaluate item performance by tracking sales and soliciting feedback. Underperforming dishes should be removed or reimagined, while successful seasonal items might be transitioned into permanent offerings. For instance, a popular fall-inspired pumpkin ravioli could remain on the menu year-round, rebranded as "Chef's Signature Ravioli."

Action Item Checklist

Design a Strategic Menu Layout:

- Identify visual hotspots on the menu, such as the top-right corner, to position high-margin dishes.
- Group items into clear categories (e.g., appetizers, mains, desserts) for better readability.
- Ensure branding is consistent with the restaurant's identity, using appropriate fonts, colors, and design elements.

Craft Compelling Menu Descriptions:

- Use sensory language to evoke taste, texture, and aroma.
- Highlight unique aspects of dishes, such as preparation methods or sourcing.
- Align descriptions with the restaurant's brand tone—playful for casual eateries, refined for upscale establishments.

Implement Psychological Pricing:

- Remove currency symbols to reduce focus on price.
- Use rounded numbers for a premium feel or .95 endings for casual environments.
- Position high-priced items strategically to influence perceived value of mid-tier options.

Leverage Seasonal and Specialty Menus:

- Design seasonal dishes using local, fresh ingredients to enhance appeal.
- Market specialty offerings as limited-time to create urgency, using phrases like "only this month" or "while supplies last."
- Promote these menus through social media, email campaigns, and partnerships with local suppliers.

Regularly Evaluate and Optimize the Menu:

- Analyze sales data to identify bestsellers and underperforming items.
- Solicit customer feedback to understand preferences and refine offerings.

- Update the menu to reflect current seasons, trends, and business goals.

Resource List

Tools:

- **Canva**: For designing visually appealing menus with customizable templates.
- **Google Analytics**: To track the effectiveness of online menu promotions.
- **Menu Engineering Software**: Programs like xtraCHEF help analyze menu performance and profitability.

Books and Reading Material:

- **"The Restaurant Manager's Handbook"** by Douglas Robert Brown: Comprehensive insights into menu design and management.
- **"Setting the Table"** by Danny Meyer: Focuses on customer experience and how menus play a role in it.

Additional Resources:

- **OpenTable Insights**: For data on customer preferences and trends.
- **Foodable Network**: Industry news and case studies for restaurant professionals.
- **Local Farmers' Networks**: For sourcing fresh, seasonal ingredients.

Integrated Summary

The chapter reveals how menus transcend their functional role to become strategic marketing assets. By applying psychological principles, crafting engaging descriptions, and keeping menus fresh with seasonal offerings, restaurants can influence customer choices, enhance the dining experience, and boost profitability. Treating the menu as a living, evolving element of the restaurant ensures it remains aligned with business goals and customer preferences, maximizing its impact in a competitive industry.

CHAPTER 5
LEVERAGING WORD-OF-MOUTH MARKETING

TURN SATISFIED CUSTOMERS INTO YOUR GREATEST ADVOCATES

Imagine walking into a local café, ordering a meal, and leaving with a recommendation so enthusiastic that your friends are compelled to visit the same spot. What started as a simple dining experience becomes an endorsement—a powerful ripple that extends far beyond the initial customer. This is the essence of word-of-mouth marketing, an age-old phenomenon now amplified by modern tools and platforms. For businesses, these genuine, unpaid endorsements are not just valuable; they are indispensable in building trust and fostering growth.

Word-of-mouth marketing thrives because it's rooted in authenticity. Unlike advertisements or promotions, it carries the weight of personal experience. When a friend or family member shares their satisfaction, they do so with credibility that no ad can replicate. This type of advocacy has been shown to drive purchasing decisions more effectively than almost any other form of marketing. According to Nielsen research, 92% of consumers trust recommendations from people they know above all other forms of advertising. For businesses, this statistic is more than just a number; it's a roadmap to creating lasting customer relationships.

The beauty of customer referrals lies in their organic nature.

People share positive experiences not because they're paid to but because they genuinely believe in the value they've received. However, the key to unlocking this potential isn't leaving it to chance; it's fostering an environment where customers feel inspired to share their experiences. This means focusing on more than just products or services—it's about delivering moments worth talking about. From exceptional service to thoughtful gestures, every interaction can turn a casual customer into a loyal advocate.

Modern businesses have endless opportunities to encourage and amplify word-of-mouth. Social media, review platforms, and referral programs provide tools to extend the reach of happy customers. A single social media post praising your business can reach hundreds, even thousands, of potential new clients. The influence doesn't end there. Online reviews, testimonials, and even casual mentions in forums or community groups become digital echoes of customer satisfaction, creating a continuous loop of advocacy.

The power of word-of-mouth marketing extends beyond acquisition; it builds a foundation of trust and community. Customers referred by others often arrive with a higher level of confidence and are more likely to become repeat patrons themselves. This cycle strengthens the connection between a business and its audience, creating relationships that are not only transactional but meaningful.

When businesses approach referrals with strategy and care, they unlock an unparalleled tool for growth. This chapter will explore how to harness word-of-mouth marketing in thoughtful and effective ways. From understanding the psychology behind customer advocacy to building systems that encourage referrals, each step will reveal how to transform satisfied customers into loyal ambassadors. In doing so, businesses don't just grow—they thrive through the voices of those they serve.

The Value of Word-of-Mouth Marketing

Why do we trust a friend's recommendation more than a flashy advertisement? The answer lies in human connection. Imagine a diner who leaves a small neighborhood restaurant so impressed by the meal that they can't wait to tell their coworkers about it. By the end of the week, several new customers walk through the door, each eager to try what they've heard described as "the best burger in town." Unlike traditional marketing, this kind of referral feels personal and authentic, carrying an impact that no paid promotion can replicate.

Word-of-mouth marketing holds power because it comes from real experiences, not polished slogans. A study by Nielsen found that 92% of consumers trust recommendations from people they know over any other form of advertising. This trust translates into action, as people are far more likely to try a business when it comes endorsed by someone they already believe. For restaurants, this effect is magnified by the emotional nature of dining. Sharing a meal is an inherently social act, and the positive feelings tied to a great experience naturally extend to the people customers talk to about it.

Restaurants that actively cultivate word-of-mouth marketing see its potential realized in many forms. Consider Chipotle's "Burrito Lovers" campaign, which rewarded customers who shared referrals with free food. This simple incentive encouraged diners to spread the word, boosting both loyalty and sales. On a smaller scale, local eateries often rely on loyal patrons to build their reputation. For example, a bakery might launch a promotion where customers who refer a friend receive a complimentary pastry, sparking excitement that ripples through the community.

The measurable impact of referrals is another reason word-of-mouth marketing is invaluable. Businesses can track metrics like the number of new customers who mention being referred by a friend or monitor increased social media activity tied to specific recommendations. Referral tracking software, such as ReferralCandy or Yotpo, allows businesses to quantify how many customers are brought in through this channel. Metrics like the lifetime value of referred customers—often significantly higher than those acquired through ads—provide insights into the long-term benefits of these efforts.

Understanding the psychology behind word-of-mouth marketing provides clarity on why it works. At its core, it's about trust and shared experiences. Customers who feel valued are more likely to share their positive stories. Creating moments that are worthy of a story, whether through outstanding service, a memorable dish, or even a unique dining atmosphere, lays the foundation for organic promotion. These experiences don't just drive immediate visits; they create lasting impressions that continue to bring new diners through the door.

The interplay of trust, authenticity, and human connection makes word-of-mouth marketing an unmatched tool for building a business. By understanding why it works, learning from successful examples, and leveraging tools to measure its impact, restaurants can tap into this age-old yet highly effective form of marketing. Through these efforts, satisfied customers transform into loyal advocates, their stories becoming the bridge that connects more people to the business.

Encouraging Customer Reviews

What compels someone to leave a glowing review of a restaurant experience? It might be the perfectly cooked steak, the kind server who went out of their way to make a child laugh, or even the simple joy of feeling seen and appreciated. Encouraging customers to share these moments online is not only an art but also a strategic necessity in today's digital landscape. Reviews are no longer an optional luxury—they're the virtual storefront of your reputation.

Asking for reviews starts with timing and authenticity. The best time to request a review is when the experience is fresh in the customer's mind, typically at the end of a meal or shortly after. A personal touch from staff members, such as a server saying, "We're so glad you enjoyed your visit—your feedback means a lot to us," can make the request feel sincere. Many restaurants use tools like follow-up emails or text messages to make the process seamless, including direct links to platforms where reviews can be posted. **The key is to make the request simple, friendly, and stress-free.**

Positive feedback doesn't happen by accident—it's the result of intentional design. The foundation lies in delivering an experience worth talking about, but subtle strategies can amplify the likelihood of a glowing review. For instance, diners who are thanked personally by a manager or owner are more likely to feel a connection and share their experience online. Offering incentives, such as a discount on the next visit or entry into a giveaway, provides a gentle nudge without feeling transactional. However, transparency is crucial—platforms like Yelp discourage monetary rewards for reviews, so focus on creative, ethical ways to encourage customer participation.

Choosing the right platforms is essential to maximizing the impact of reviews. Google is a universal starting point, as it directly influences search rankings and visibility. Yelp remains a powerhouse for restaurants, especially for local discovery. Social platforms like Facebook also play a role, particularly in building trust among community networks. **The right platform depends on your audience—knowing where they already engage helps direct your efforts.** For upscale dining, platforms like TripAdvisor may carry more weight, while casual eateries might benefit most from Google or Facebook.

Understanding the metrics behind customer reviews adds depth to their value. Tracking the average rating, the number of reviews, and their recency paints a picture of your restaurant's digital health. Responding to reviews, both positive and negative, shows prospective customers that you care about feedback. Data from BrightLocal reveals that 88% of consumers trust online reviews as much as personal recommendations, making active management of your reputation a non-negotiable task.

Encouraging reviews is about more than asking—it's about creating a culture where feedback is natural and appreciated. When customers feel that their opinion truly matters, they're more likely to take the time to share it. Whether through small acts of gratitude, streamlined tools, or cultivating a standout experience, every effort contributes to a digital presence that mirrors your restaurant's commitment to excellence. In today's world, where online opinions often precede dining decisions, encouraging customer reviews is not just wise—it's essential.

Creating Shareable Experiences

"People don't share boring." This simple yet profound insight from Seth Godin's *Purple Cow* encapsulates the essence of creating shareable experiences. In a crowded market, standing out isn't optional—it's survival. Restaurants that generate buzz understand this principle and design every element of their ambiance and service to captivate guests and inspire conversation. These experiences become more than a meal; they transform into stories diners are eager to tell.

Ambiance is where the magic begins. A restaurant's design, lighting, and music work together to shape how guests feel from the moment they step inside. Imagine a café where neon signs glow with witty phrases against a backdrop of hand-painted murals. These elements make the space instantly Instagram-worthy, encouraging guests to snap photos and tag the location. Research shows that 49% of diners discover restaurants through social media posts from friends, making every shareable moment a potential marketing boost.

Service is equally powerful in fostering organic buzz. Exceptional service goes beyond efficiency; it creates personal connections. Consider the impact of a server who remembers a regular guest's favorite drink or a chef who stops by to explain the inspiration behind a dish. These thoughtful touches leave lasting impressions, prompting guests to share their experiences online or with friends. **What feels like a small gesture can often turn into a story that spreads far beyond the restaurant's walls.**

Remarkable experiences are intentional, not accidental. Borrowing from *Purple Cow's* philosophy, restaurants should focus on offering something so unique it demands attention. Think of the allure of themed restaurants where the décor, menu, and even staff uniforms create a cohesive, unforgettable experience. A speakeasy-style bar hidden behind a bookcase or a dessert served in a miniature smoking cauldron are memorable details that encourage sharing. These standout features not only attract guests but also give them a reason to talk about their visit.

Visual appeal plays a significant role in making moments shareable. Restaurants with bold, eye-catching features—such as a colorful flower wall, a rooftop with skyline views, or tableside cooking demonstrations—naturally draw attention. Diners are more likely to post about meals that feel special or visually striking. **Photos of a stunning dish plated with artistic flair or a whimsical cocktail topped with edible flowers create instant online buzz, turning diners into unofficial brand ambassadors.**

Creating unforgettable dining experiences goes beyond aesthetics. The emotional connection guests form during their visit often determines whether they'll share it. Moments of delight, such as a complimentary amuse-bouche or a heartfelt note included with the check, make guests feel valued. These thoughtful surprises are small investments that yield substantial returns in word-of-mouth promotion. For example, a family celebrating a birthday might find their dessert arrives with sparklers and a handwritten card, turning a routine outing into a cherished memory.

When designed thoughtfully, these experiences don't just appeal to the senses—they reflect the restaurant's identity. A cozy bistro might focus on intimate, candlelit tables and personal service, while a bustling brunch spot could feature vibrant colors, playful décor, and a menu filled with creative twists. Authenticity matters. Shareable experiences work best when they align seamlessly with the brand's character, ensuring that every story shared reinforces the restaurant's unique appeal.

Fostering shareable moments requires both creativity and strategy. From ambiance to service, every detail must work together to create an environment that feels effortless yet remarkable. In a world where dining out often starts with scrolling through social media, the ability to create buzzworthy experiences is no longer optional—it's essential for standing out and building lasting connections with guests.

Rewarding Loyal Customers and Advocates

"Loyalty is not won by being first. It is won by being best." This quote from Stew Leonard, founder of the famed grocery chain known for its exceptional customer retention, captures the essence of rewarding loyal customers and advocates. In the competitive world of hospitality, where experiences are fleeting but impressions last, creating programs that both reward and encourage advocacy transforms occasional diners into lifelong patrons.

Loyalty programs are the cornerstone of incentivizing referrals. These systems reward consistent engagement, giving customers a tangible reason to return while creating opportunities for them to share their positive experiences. For example, a restaurant might introduce a program where diners earn points for every visit, which can be redeemed for discounts or exclusive perks. To amplify the impact, these programs often integrate referral rewards, such as granting additional points when a loyal customer brings in a new guest. **This creates a feedback loop where loyalty leads to advocacy, and advocacy fosters loyalty, driving growth from both directions.**

Recognizing and celebrating repeat customers goes beyond transactional rewards. People value acknowledgment, especially in spaces where they've invested time and money. Simple gestures, like addressing repeat diners by name or offering a complimentary appetizer to mark their 10th visit, make guests feel appreciated and reinforce their connection to the brand. **Personalization adds depth to these interactions. Remembering a regular's favorite drink or their usual table transforms the dining experience into a partnership, not just a purchase.**

Referral rewards can take many forms, but the most effective programs are easy to use and clearly communicated. A system offering $10 off for both the referrer and the referred diner, for example, creates immediate incentives on both sides. Digital integration, such as mobile apps or email links, streamlines the process, making participation effortless. Restaurants can also layer exclusivity into these programs by introducing limited-time referral bonuses, encouraging swift action. **The more intuitive and rewarding the system, the higher the likelihood of participation, resulting in organic growth fueled by your most passionate customers.**

Implementing and promoting these systems requires thoughtful planning. An ideal starting point is understanding the behaviors and preferences of your audience. For a casual dining spot with a young, tech-savvy demographic, app-based loyalty and referral systems may resonate best. On the other hand, fine dining establishments may benefit from invitation-only loyalty programs that emphasize exclusivity, such as access to special menus or private events. **Aligning the program's structure with the brand's identity ensures it feels authentic and appealing to its intended audience.**

Effective promotion is just as important as the program itself. Digital tools such as email campaigns and social media posts spread the word quickly, especially when paired with visuals that emphasize the benefits. For example, a promotional graphic showcasing a family enjoying a complimentary meal through a loyalty program connects emotionally with potential participants. In-store signage, such as table tents or QR codes on receipts, captures the attention of existing customers at the point of engagement, nudging them to enroll on the spot. **A comprehensive communication strategy ensures the program is not only noticed but also understood, maximizing its reach and impact.**

Measuring the success of loyalty and referral programs requires consistent tracking of key metrics. Metrics such as repeat visit rates, referral conversion percentages, and overall revenue growth tied to the program offer insights into its effectiveness. Restaurants can adjust their strategies based on these findings, such as introducing new tiers for rewards or adjusting point values to align better with customer behavior. **Data-driven refinement ensures the program evolves alongside the needs of its audience, maintaining its relevance and appeal.**

Ultimately, rewarding loyal customers and advocates is about building relationships that extend beyond a single meal.

Programs that combine thoughtful incentives with personalized recognition foster a sense of belonging, turning customers into ambassadors who champion the brand both online and offline. These initiatives are investments not just in retention but in creating a dining experience that customers are proud to share and recommend. When done well, they create a self-sustaining cycle of loyalty, advocacy, and growth, proving that a little appreciation can lead to enduring success.

Application of Techniques: Leveraging Word-of-Mouth Marketing for Growth

Understanding the Power of Word-of-Mouth: The core of word-of-mouth marketing lies in authenticity. Personal recommendations from trusted sources are perceived as credible and carry unmatched persuasive power. Restaurants, for instance, can enhance this effect by providing exceptional service and memorable experiences, ensuring customers leave with stories worth sharing.

For example, a neighborhood bakery could implement a promotion like "Refer a Friend and Both Get a Free Cookie." Such campaigns not only encourage referrals but also align with the natural act of sharing food, enhancing emotional connections.

Creating Shareable Experiences: Experiences must be designed to evoke genuine delight. Ambiance, thoughtful gestures, and unique offerings are key elements that inspire customers to share their experiences both online and offline. A rooftop bar with spectacular skyline views, for instance, becomes a destination for Instagram-worthy moments, translating customer satisfaction into organic promotions.

Applying Seth Godin's "Purple Cow" principle—offering something so unique it demands attention—restaurants can create standout features. This might include an interactive dessert menu where guests assemble their own treats, providing both a memorable experience and a reason to share.

Encouraging Reviews: Customer reviews function as modern testimonials, shaping perceptions and influencing decisions. To encourage feedback, businesses should make the process simple and rewarding. A restaurant could send follow-up emails with direct links to review platforms like Google or Yelp, paired with a friendly message: "We loved hosting you! Share your thoughts and help others discover us."

Incentivizing reviews ethically—such as offering a discount on a future visit—further encourages participation. Transparency is essential, as deceptive practices can backfire and harm credibility.

Rewarding Advocates and Repeat Customers: Loyalty programs strengthen relationships by recognizing repeat customers. For example, a café might offer points for each visit, redeemable for free drinks or exclusive menu items. These programs should also integrate referral incentives, creating a symbiotic cycle where loyalty begets advocacy and vice versa.

Restaurants can also personalize their recognition efforts. Remembering a customer's favorite dish or celebrating milestones like birthdays with small perks ensures patrons feel valued, increasing their likelihood to return and recommend the establishment to others.

Leveraging Digital Platforms: Modern tools amplify word-of-mouth marketing. Social media posts, review platforms, and referral apps extend the reach of happy customers. For example, a restaurant can run a "Share and Win" campaign on Instagram, offering participants a chance to win a meal voucher for posting a photo from their visit. Platforms like ReferralCandy simplify tracking referral success, allowing businesses to quantify the impact of their efforts.

Action Item Checklist

Design a Memorable Ambiance:

- Invest in unique décor and lighting that aligns with your brand identity.
- Incorporate features like a photo-worthy mural or a signature dish presentation.

Deliver Thoughtful Service:

- Train staff to personalize interactions, such as remembering regulars' preferences.
- Add small gestures like handwritten thank-you notes or complimentary tasters.

Simplify the Review Process:

- Provide links to platforms like Google and Yelp via follow-up emails or QR codes.
- Use signage to remind customers to leave reviews.

Monitor and Respond:

- Actively manage reviews, addressing negative feedback constructively.

Develop a Rewards System:

- Offer tiered rewards to keep customers engaged over time.
- Include referral incentives to encourage advocates.

Personalize Recognition:

- Celebrate milestones, such as the 10th visit or birthdays, with small perks.

Run Social Media Campaigns:

- Encourage user-generated content with contests and branded hashtags.

Track Referral Metrics:

- Use software like ReferralCandy to measure the impact of word-of-mouth campaigns.

Adapt Based on Data:

- Refine programs based on feedback and performance analytics.

Resource List

Tools:

- **ReferralCandy:** Tracks referrals, measures success, and simplifies incentive distribution.
- **Yelp for Business:** Optimizes your restaurant's presence on Yelp, increasing visibility and credibility.
- **Canva:** Creates engaging graphics for promoting campaigns and encouraging reviews.

Books and Reading Material:

- **"Purple Cow" by Seth Godin** - Explores how businesses can stand out in a crowded market.
- **"Contagious: How Things Catch On" by Jonah Berger -** Offers insights into why people share and how to create shareable content.

Additional Resources:

Online Courses: Coursera's "Viral Marketing and How to Craft Contagious Content."

Forums and Communities: Reddit's r/Entrepreneur for sharing real-world business experiences.

CHAPTER 6
TRACKING AND MEASURING MARKETING SUCCESS

USE DATA TO IMPROVE AND SCALE YOUR MARKETING EFFORTS

Data is the language of growth. Imagine running a campaign that feels groundbreaking, only to discover later it missed the mark entirely. Without knowing where you stand or what works, making decisions about marketing becomes guesswork. Tracking and measuring success provides clarity, enabling businesses to adapt and thrive in an ever-changing landscape. It turns subjective guesses into actionable insights, offering a roadmap for smarter strategies.

Understanding what works in marketing is less about intuition and more about evidence. Businesses often spend resources on ads, social media, and content creation without knowing which of these efforts truly connects with their audience. Measurement tools, like analytics platforms, help identify patterns that would otherwise go unnoticed. For instance, tracking website visits after an email campaign might reveal which messages resonate most, giving businesses a way to double down on what matters.

The benefits extend beyond spotting trends. Measurement uncovers inefficiencies, showing where energy and budgets are being wasted. A marketing team might assume their strongest asset is paid search ads, but data could reveal that referrals or organic social media posts drive better results at a fraction of the cost. By identifying these blind spots, businesses can reallocate resources more effectively, focusing on efforts that yield the highest returns.

More than just a scorecard, tracking also provides a window into customer behavior. Every click, like, or visit tells a story about what people value. A bakery may notice that posts about seasonal items like pumpkin spice desserts generate higher engagement than their other offerings. Insights like these allow businesses to craft campaigns and products tailored to customer desires, ensuring their message aligns with their audience's expectations.

The importance of measuring results doesn't stop at understanding past performance. It enables businesses to forecast and plan for the future. By monitoring customer trends, a restaurant might predict when to introduce a new menu item or adjust their advertising strategy before a seasonal rush. This forward-thinking approach turns raw data into actionable foresight, offering a competitive edge.

Ultimately, tracking and measuring success isn't about collecting numbers for the sake of it. It's about using those numbers to refine every step of the marketing process. Whether it's spotting trends, cutting waste, or anticipating future needs, measurement is the foundation upon which better decisions are built. This chapter will explore how businesses can turn data into action, unlocking growth by working smarter, not harder.

Why Metrics Matter in Marketing

Why do some marketing efforts succeed while others fall flat? The answer often lies in the metrics—or lack thereof. Consider a small café that spends heavily on online ads, only to see little change in foot traffic. Frustrated, the owner decides to try a new approach: tracking the effectiveness of each ad by monitoring clicks, customer inquiries, and actual purchases. Within weeks, patterns emerge. Ads featuring seasonal pastries drive far more visits than those promoting generic menu items. This data not only reshapes the café's marketing focus but also prevents future wasteful spending. Tracking performance isn't just about numbers; it's about understanding what works and making informed decisions.

Metrics matter because they provide clarity. In marketing, guessing can be costly. Data-driven insights replace uncertainty with precision, allowing businesses to pinpoint their most effective strategies. For instance, a restaurant might believe that social media is its strongest driver of reservations. However, tracking reveals that while social media generates plenty of interest, it's email marketing that consistently converts interest into bookings. Insights like these allow businesses to double down on what delivers results.

Yet, measuring success isn't without its challenges. Many businesses struggle to decide which metrics matter most or how to interpret the data they collect. A common issue is relying on surface-level numbers without digging deeper. Take website traffic as an example. High traffic might seem like a win, but if visitors aren't converting into customers, the real issue lies elsewhere. Misinterpreting such data can lead businesses to chase vanity metrics—figures that look impressive but offer little actual value. Understanding the difference between metrics that inform action and those that merely boost morale is critical to meaningful analysis.

Key performance indicators (KPIs) help businesses focus on what truly matters. For restaurants, metrics like reservation rates, average order value, and repeat customer frequency are far more telling than the number of Instagram likes. **Monitoring**

these metrics reveals both strengths and weaknesses, enabling targeted improvements. For example, if repeat visits are low, the issue might lie in customer experience rather than marketing. This insight allows a business to direct resources toward creating loyalty programs or enhancing service, rather than pouring more money into ads.

Modern tools simplify the process of collecting and analyzing data. Customer relationship management (CRM) systems track everything from purchase history to feedback, while analytics platforms reveal trends in website activity or social media engagement. Pairing these tools with clear goals ensures businesses not only collect data but also use it effectively. For instance, by integrating a CRM with a loyalty program, a restaurant can identify its top-spending customers and offer them tailored promotions, further boosting their lifetime value.

Measuring success also fosters accountability. When data drives decisions, marketing efforts can be justified with evidence rather than assumptions. A restaurant that notices a decline in online reviews can address the issue directly, whether it's improving service or revamping the menu. Without tracking, these opportunities for improvement would likely go unnoticed, leading to stagnation rather than growth.

Metrics are the foundation of smart marketing. By focusing on the right ones and using them to guide decisions, businesses transform raw data into actionable insights. This approach not only improves individual campaigns but also builds a culture of continual learning and refinement, ensuring sustained success in a competitive market.

Tools for Measuring Marketing Effectiveness

What separates successful marketing campaigns from those that fall short? Often, the answer lies in the tools used to measure their impact. In the restaurant industry, where margins are tight and competition is fierce, understanding how to track and interpret marketing performance can mean the difference between thriving and merely surviving. Tools that provide actionable insights transform guesswork into strategy, allowing businesses to focus their resources where they matter most.

Google Analytics is one of the most powerful tools available for monitoring website performance, yet many businesses fail to unlock its full potential. Setting it up is straightforward but requires attention to detail. Begin by creating a Google Analytics account and linking it to your website through a unique tracking code. This code collects data on user behavior, including how visitors find your site, how long they stay, and which pages they view. With this information, restaurants can identify their most effective marketing channels. For instance, if the data reveals that most traffic comes from Instagram, it underscores the value of investing in visual content and social media ads.

Customizing reports in Google Analytics ensures that the insights are tailored to your needs. For a restaurant, key metrics might include the number of reservations made through the site, the average time spent on the menu page, or the bounce rate—how quickly visitors leave after arriving. By setting goals within the platform, such as tracking completed reservation forms, businesses can measure the direct impact of their marketing efforts on revenue.

Social media platforms come with their own built-in analytics tools, offering another layer of insight. Facebook Insights and Instagram Analytics, for example, provide data on audience engagement, reach, and demographics. These tools help restaurants understand who their customers are and how they interact with content. Suppose a brunch café notices that posts featuring customer testimonials receive higher engagement than promotional ads. This observation suggests a shift in strategy—highlighting customer stories to build trust and encourage more organic interactions.

To dig deeper into social media performance, consider using tools like Hootsuite or Sprout Social. These platforms consolidate data from multiple channels, making it easier to spot trends and compare the effectiveness of campaigns across platforms. For example, a fine dining restaurant might notice that their Instagram Stories generate more clicks than their Facebook posts. Armed with this knowledge, they can prioritize content creation for the platform that delivers better results.

Paid tools such as HubSpot or SEMrush expand beyond basic tracking to offer advanced features like competitor analysis and keyword tracking. These tools are particularly valuable for restaurants aiming to improve their search engine rankings. By identifying which keywords drive traffic to competitors, businesses can adjust their own content to capture more search volume. For example, if "best rooftop dining in town" ranks high for a rival restaurant, creating blog posts or social media campaigns around that phrase could help attract similar audiences.

Challenges often arise when trying to interpret the flood of data these tools provide. The key is to focus on actionable metrics rather than getting lost in the details. A restaurant doesn't need to monitor every number but should prioritize those directly tied to business goals. If increasing weekday reservations is the objective, then tracking clicks on reservation links and their conversion rates becomes the priority. This focus ensures that every marketing decision is data-backed and aligned with overarching objectives.

Leveraging tools for marketing effectiveness is not about adopting every solution available but rather using the right tools for your specific goals. For restaurants, this means combining website analytics, social media insights, and industry-specific platforms to create a comprehensive view of what drives success. When implemented with purpose, these tools offer clarity and direction, helping businesses allocate their resources wisely and achieve measurable growth.

Analyzing and Interpreting Results

"Data is only as valuable as the decisions it inspires." This insight captures the essence of analyzing marketing performance. Numbers alone don't drive success; the meaning drawn from them does. When you begin to uncover patterns in customer behavior or see the direct impact of a campaign on reservations, what once seemed abstract becomes the roadmap to actionable strategies. It's this shift—from raw metrics to meaningful insights—that separates reactive marketing from intentional growth.

The first step in turning data into actionable insights lies in understanding what to look for. Imagine a restaurant promoting a new brunch menu. Metrics such as increased website visits, higher engagement on Instagram posts, and a rise in mid-morning reservations might seem encouraging at a glance. Yet, these numbers mean little without context. Did reservations increase because of the promotion or due to a nearby event driving traffic to the area? Connecting cause to effect requires narrowing focus to data that reflects direct impacts, such as tracking how many clicks on the brunch ad led to reservation confirmations. **Key performance indicators (KPIs), like click-through rates and conversion rates, become invaluable for answering these questions.**

Patterns in customer behavior often reveal opportunities and weaknesses that aren't immediately obvious. For example, a café might notice through Google Analytics that most visitors leave their website after viewing the menu page. This could indicate confusion about pricing or that essential details like operating hours are missing. Addressing these gaps—by updating the menu layout or adding a call-to-action for reservations—turns potential lost customers into seated diners. Similarly, monitoring social media activity might show that posts featuring behind-the-scenes content consistently outperform promotional ads. Recognizing this pattern enables a shift in strategy to produce more of what customers clearly value.

Adjusting strategies based on performance data demands both adaptability and a clear process. For instance, a fine-dining restaurant launching a prix fixe dinner might initially advertise it across multiple platforms. However, analytics reveal that email campaigns drive higher bookings than Facebook ads. Rather than continue to spread resources thin, the team redirects efforts toward refining their email strategy, perhaps by testing different subject lines or segmenting their audience for personalized offers. **This approach—testing, learning, and refining—creates a feedback loop that steadily improves marketing outcomes over time.**

Challenges in interpreting data often stem from trying to analyze too much at once. It's easy to feel overwhelmed when staring at a dashboard filled with metrics, each vying for attention. Focusing on the KPIs that align with specific goals is the antidote. A fast-casual restaurant aiming to boost lunch traffic might track metrics like order frequency between 11 a.m. and 2 p.m. or the effectiveness of a loyalty program during that time frame. Eliminating distractions helps maintain clarity and ensures that adjustments address the right problems.

To ensure data leads to actionable steps, it's essential to evaluate performance regularly and consistently. Weekly reviews provide a cadence for spotting emerging trends, while quarterly deep dives allow for evaluating long-term impacts. Combining short-term snapshots with a broader view creates a complete picture of performance. For example, short-term metrics may show a spike in sales following a seasonal promotion, while long-term analysis might reveal whether those new customers became repeat diners.

Finally, drawing insights from data works best when shared collaboratively across teams. A server might notice patterns in customer preferences that don't show up in digital analytics. Combining their observations with online data enriches understanding and fosters a culture of learning. When teams work together to analyze results, they're better equipped to design strategies that address the complete customer experience, from digital engagement to in-person service.

Through careful analysis, pattern recognition, and thoughtful adaptation, data becomes a living resource, not just a static report. When businesses use these insights to guide their decisions, they unlock the full potential of their marketing efforts and move toward sustained growth.

Scaling Your Marketing Efforts

"Success leaves clues." This statement, often attributed to Tony Robbins, encapsulates the essence of scaling marketing efforts. The strategies that yield consistent results, the campaigns that outperform expectations, and the insights that align with customer behavior—all point the way to scalable growth. But scaling is more than repeating past success; it requires reinvestment, strategic refinement, and preparing for the inevitable challenges of growth.

Scaling begins with identifying strategies that consistently outperform. For instance, a neighborhood bistro running a weekday happy hour promotion notices that social media ads targeting nearby office workers generate a high volume of reservations. Instead of simply replicating this strategy, scaling involves enhancing its scope. **Expanding the budget for these ads, testing new messaging formats, or even introducing a referral incentive for group bookings amplifies what is already working.** The goal is to transition from isolated successes to a comprehensive system that sustains growth over time.

Reinvesting profits is a critical component of scaling. Too often, businesses become complacent, allocating minimal resources to marketing once they see positive returns. Yet, the most successful enterprises treat their marketing budgets as dynamic tools for growth. For example, a fine-dining restaurant experiencing a surge in reservations after partnering with influencers might reinvest part of the profits into additional collaborations with micro-influencers who align with their target demographic. **This reinvestment not only increases reach but also allows the restaurant to refine its approach by learning from each campaign's performance data.**

Preparing for future marketing growth requires more than capital; it demands infrastructure. As campaigns scale, so do the complexities of managing them. A small café that relies on manual tracking for its loyalty program may find this approach unsustainable as its customer base expands. Investing in scalable tools—such as CRM software to manage customer relationships or automated marketing platforms to handle email campaigns—ensures that the growth doesn't overwhelm operational capacity. **The ability to automate repetitive tasks frees up resources to focus on strategy and innovation, essential components of sustained growth.**

Recognizing market shifts and adapting to them is another pillar of scaling. What works in one season or with one audience segment may not yield the same results over time. Seasonal restaurants, for example, often rely on targeted ads during their peak months but can scale their efforts by introducing off-season promotions. Partnering with local event organizers to host winter pop-ups or collaborating on bundled experiences with nearby attractions allows for sustained engagement, even during slower periods. **Scaling efforts should account for these fluctuations, ensuring growth remains steady year-round.** Data continues to play a pivotal role as marketing efforts scale. Tracking performance metrics across campaigns becomes even more critical, as larger-scale initiatives can quickly drain resources if not optimized. A quick-service restaurant chain expanding into new markets might leverage geotargeted advertising, comparing performance across regions to refine its approach. **Analyzing data at this level reveals opportunities for localized adjustments, such as tailoring messaging to reflect regional preferences or adjusting promotional offers to match local demand.**

Scaling also requires a mindset shift from reactive to proactive marketing. Rather than waiting for trends or opportunities to emerge, forward-thinking businesses anticipate them. For example, a farm-to-table restaurant predicting a surge in demand for sustainable dining might develop content and campaigns highlighting its sourcing practices long before competitors catch on. **This proactive approach positions the business as a leader in the space, attracting attention and building momentum before others can respond.**

Sustainability in scaling efforts hinges on balance. Aggressive expansion without a clear strategy often leads to diminishing returns or operational burnout. On the other hand, overly cautious approaches risk leaving growth opportunities untapped. Successful scaling balances ambition with foresight, reinvestment with sustainability, and innovation with consistency. By identifying winning strategies, reinvesting wisely, and preparing for the complexities of growth, businesses create a foundation that supports not just expansion, but enduring success.

Application of Techniques: Tracking and Measuring Marketing Success

Identifying Winning Strategies to Scale: Scaling begins with pinpointing what works and refining it for broader application. For example, consider a neighborhood café that notices its Instagram promotions for seasonal drinks drive the highest traffic. This insight can be used to scale efforts by expanding the ad budget for similar posts or promoting them on multiple platforms like Facebook or TikTok. Testing different visuals or call-to-actions while maintaining the seasonal theme helps optimize results. **The essence of this approach lies in learning from past successes to ensure resources are directed toward initiatives with proven outcomes.**

Reinvesting Profits into High-Performing Channels: Reinvestment is a critical step in scaling. Let's say a fine-dining restaurant experiences a 15% boost in reservations after a partnership with a local food blogger. Instead of considering this a one-off success, the restaurant could reinvest profits into partnerships with other influencers or bloggers who share a similar audience. This also applies to online ads. A high-performing Google Ads campaign targeting "romantic dinners in the city" might warrant additional investment to test broader keywords like "date night restaurants." **The key is to reallocate funds into campaigns and tools that yield measurable returns, ensuring every dollar works harder for the business.**

Preparing for Future Growth: Infrastructure plays an essential role as marketing efforts scale. A small café relying on manual social media updates might quickly become overwhelmed as campaigns expand. Investing in automation tools like Hootsuite or Buffer ensures posts are scheduled consistently across platforms, saving time while maintaining engagement. For customer relationships, a restaurant could implement a CRM tool to track top spenders and send them personalized promotions. **This scalability ensures operational efficiency while maintaining the quality and consistency of marketing efforts.**

Recognizing and Adapting to Market Shifts: Market dynamics are fluid, requiring a proactive approach to adapt. Seasonal restaurants might notice that traffic wanes after peak months. To maintain visibility, they could launch winter campaigns, such as discounted holiday-themed menus or collaborations with local event organizers for pop-up experiences. For example, an ice cream parlor might introduce hot chocolate kits in the colder months to sustain customer interest. **Adjusting strategies based on external factors not only extends relevance but also creates new revenue streams.**

Leveraging Data to Optimize Scaling Efforts: Scaling requires a deeper focus on data-driven decisions. For instance, a quick-service restaurant expanding into new regions can use geotargeted ads to compare engagement and conversion rates across locations. This granular analysis allows adjustments to be made, such as customizing messaging for each region or shifting focus to higher-performing areas. **As campaigns grow, detailed metrics ensure that resources are spent on the most impactful strategies.**

Action Item Checklist

Identify High-Performing Campaigns:

- Review past campaign metrics to identify top performers.
- Evaluate KPIs such as ROI, customer engagement, and conversion rates.
- Note the common elements (e.g., messaging, visuals, audience targeting) of successful campaigns.

Reallocate Marketing Budget:

- Reinvest profits into scaling high-performing campaigns.
- Allocate funds to test variations of winning strategies (e.g., new platforms or additional keywords).

Implement Scalable Tools:

- Invest in CRM software to manage customer data and interactions efficiently.
- Use automation tools for scheduling and managing content across multiple platforms.

Monitor and Adapt to Market Trends:

- Analyze seasonal trends and create marketing plans for off-peak periods.
- Collaborate with local businesses or events to introduce creative promotions.

Refine Campaigns with Data Insights:

- Use analytics tools to measure performance at a granular level (e.g., by location, audience segment).
- Test A/B variations of ads to identify the most effective content.

Prepare for Long-Term Growth:

- Develop infrastructure to handle increased marketing volume without sacrificing quality.

- Train teams on using advanced marketing tools and interpreting performance data.

Regularly Evaluate and Adjust Strategies:

- Schedule quarterly reviews to assess the effectiveness of scaling efforts.
- Adjust strategies based on feedback, new data, or changing market conditions.

Resource List

Tools:

- **Google Analytics:** For tracking website traffic and conversion metrics, essential for identifying high-performing campaigns.
- **Hootsuite/Buffer:** Social media automation tools to manage content efficiently across platforms.
- **HubSpot:** A robust CRM for tracking customer interactions and automating personalized marketing.
- **Sprout Social:** To consolidate social media analytics and measure engagement across channels.

Books and Reading Material:

- *Restaurant Marketing for Owners and Managers* by David Pavesic – A practical guide to understanding restaurant-specific marketing strategies and how to implement them effectively.
- *Contagious: How to Build Word of Mouth in the Digital Age* by Jonah Berger – Explores how ideas and

products gain traction, offering insights relevant to scaling campaigns.

Additional Resources:

- Online Course: *Digital Marketing Specialization* by the University of Illinois (Coursera) – Offers in-depth training on marketing analytics and campaign optimization.
- Website: *MarketingProfs* – A hub for actionable marketing advice, tools, and insights tailored for small businesses.

CHAPTER 7
AVOIDING COMMON MARKETING MISTAKES

LEARN WHAT NOT TO DO TO PROTECT YOUR REPUTATION AND BUDGET

Marketing can feel like navigating a maze without a map when mistakes go unnoticed or unchecked. A business may launch a flashy campaign or invest heavily in a new platform, only to discover that their efforts have missed the mark. While it's easy to focus on what to do in marketing, understanding what not to do can often make the difference between wasted effort and lasting success. Avoiding common mistakes isn't just about protecting your budget—it's about preserving your reputation and building trust with your audience.

Marketing pitfalls often stem from assumptions rather than insights. For example, a small restaurant might assume that offering steep discounts will drive traffic, only to find that it attracts one-time bargain hunters rather than loyal patrons. Similarly, a brand might prioritize a trending platform like TikTok without asking if it aligns with their target audience. Missteps like these can lead to campaigns that fail to deliver value, draining both time and resources. Recognizing and avoiding these errors ensures that every decision is grounded in purpose and strategy.

Mistakes in marketing can also ripple outward, impacting customer perception in ways that are hard to undo. Imagine a café that over-promotes a new dessert, only to run out of stock when demand peaks. Disappointed customers may leave with a negative impression that no follow-up campaign can erase. By planning for contingencies and understanding potential challenges, businesses can mitigate risks before they escalate. Avoiding these errors builds a stronger foundation for customer trust and long-term growth.

Many marketing missteps occur because businesses fail to track or measure their efforts effectively. Without clear data, it's easy to double down on strategies that aren't working or ignore opportunities hiding in plain sight. For instance, a bakery might continue to post daily on social media without realizing that email campaigns yield far better engagement. By learning from these scenarios, businesses can avoid repeating the same costly errors and instead focus on what truly drives results.

Mistakes don't just drain budgets; they cost businesses valuable time. Repeating avoidable errors means lost opportunities to connect with the right audience or fine-tune a message that resonates. A focus on recognizing common pitfalls allows businesses to reclaim this time and redirect it toward thoughtful strategies that align with their goals. By identifying the gaps in planning, execution, or measurement, businesses can take proactive steps toward success.

This chapter explores how to identify and sidestep the most frequent marketing errors, providing a framework for smarter decision-making. From recognizing misplaced priorities to understanding the unintended consequences of misaligned campaigns, the insights shared here will help businesses build strategies that avoid pitfalls and maximize outcomes. Mistakes may be inevitable in any field, but learning to anticipate and address them turns potential setbacks into opportunities for refinement and growth.

Understanding Common Marketing Errors

Imagine a bustling café launching an expensive ad campaign to promote a new seasonal drink. The advertisements are everywhere—social media, local newspapers, even posters on nearby streets. Yet, weeks later, sales numbers show the drink hasn't gained traction. What went wrong? A deeper dive reveals the campaign used language that didn't connect with the target audience, leaving them uninterested. This oversight highlights one of the most frequent errors in restaurant marketing: assuming a message resonates without understanding the audience.

One of the most common mistakes is overpromising and underdelivering. For example, restaurants often use phrases like "Best Pizza in Town" or "Award-Winning Burgers" without the accolades or unique quality to back them up. When diners arrive with high expectations and experience an average meal, they're not just disappointed—they're likely to share their dissatisfaction online. **This kind of misstep damages both brand image and future sales, as trust is a cornerstone of customer loyalty.**

Another frequent pitfall is ignoring customer feedback. A family-owned diner might receive comments that their menu lacks vegetarian options but chooses to dismiss the suggestion, assuming their customer base doesn't care about such offerings. Over time, this decision limits the restaurant's appeal and alienates a growing demographic. **Listening to and acting on feedback is one of the simplest ways to prevent revenue loss and foster a sense of community with patrons.**

Mismanaging promotions can also hurt a business. A steakhouse might advertise a "Buy One Get One Free" deal but fail to account for the cost of goods sold. If the influx of customers during the promotion leads to financial losses, the campaign does more harm than good. Worse, running out of ingredients or overloading staff can frustrate diners, who might not return. **Proper planning ensures promotions deliver value without compromising quality or operations.**

Neglecting the power of consistent branding is another mistake that impacts revenue and customer recognition. A high-end restaurant posting casual, meme-style content on its social media can confuse potential diners about its identity. Conversely, a casual eatery using overly formal language may seem unapproachable. **Maintaining alignment between your brand's personality and how you market it creates clarity, helping customers feel confident in their choices.**

Errors in marketing don't just harm a restaurant's immediate sales—they have a ripple effect on long-term growth. Poorly targeted ads or mismatched branding waste budgets that could have been used to build effective strategies. Mistakes also make it harder to measure what works, leading businesses to repeat the same missteps instead of refining their efforts. **This cycle erodes both resources and morale, creating unnecessary hurdles to success.**

Avoiding these pitfalls requires a commitment to strategy and reflection. By ensuring marketing aligns with the brand, resonates with the audience, and reflects operational realities, restaurants can safeguard their reputation while maximizing impact. The key lies in understanding the direct consequences of common errors, using those insights to create smarter campaigns that foster trust, loyalty, and sustainable growth.

Misaligning Goals and Campaigns

Why do so many marketing campaigns fail to deliver results despite significant time and resources invested? The answer often lies in misaligned goals. A high-end restaurant, for instance, might launch a sleek digital ad campaign to attract new diners but measure success based solely on social media engagement. While likes and comments may soar, these metrics do little to boost actual reservations or revenue. This disconnect between the goal and the campaign's focus illustrates how unclear objectives lead to wasted efforts and missed opportunities.

When goals and campaigns are out of sync, businesses often find themselves chasing the wrong metrics. Imagine a bakery aiming to increase weekday foot traffic but dedicating its entire advertising budget to Instagram posts showcasing elaborate weekend brunches. While the posts may generate excitement, they fail to address the bakery's primary objective of drawing customers during quieter hours. **Aligning campaigns with clear, measurable goals is critical to ensuring that every marketing dollar contributes to the desired outcome.**

A crucial step in avoiding this pitfall is establishing precise objectives before crafting a campaign. Broad aims such as "increase brand awareness" or "boost sales" are too vague to guide effective strategy. Instead, breaking these down into specific, actionable goals—like "grow weekday reservations by 20% within three months" or "double loyalty program sign-ups this quarter"—provides a clear direction. **Specific goals not only clarify the campaign's purpose but also serve as benchmarks for evaluating success.**

Once goals are defined, aligning them with the right strategies becomes essential. For instance, a fast-casual restaurant looking to enhance lunch sales might invest in targeted digital ads that offer discounts redeemable between 11 a.m. and 2 p.m. These campaigns focus directly on driving traffic during a specific time frame, ensuring alignment with the restaurant's objective. Conversely, promoting a dinner special in the same ads would dilute the impact, wasting resources on messaging that doesn't match the goal.

Maintaining this alignment requires consistent monitoring

and adjustment. Tools like Google Analytics and customer relationship management (CRM) platforms are invaluable in tracking performance against goals. A café might use analytics to measure how many website visitors click through a "Lunch Specials" ad and ultimately place an order. If the numbers fall short, refining the ad's messaging or adjusting the target audience can improve outcomes. **These tools provide actionable insights that keep campaigns on track, preventing misalignment from derailing progress.**

Equally important is ensuring that everyone involved in a campaign understands its purpose. Marketing teams, front-of-house staff, and even suppliers should share a unified vision of the campaign's goals. A fine-dining restaurant promoting a limited-time wine pairing menu, for example, needs its servers to highlight the offering during dinner service. This cohesion ensures that the campaign's impact extends beyond digital spaces to the customer's actual experience, creating a seamless alignment between marketing and operations.

One overlooked aspect of maintaining alignment is accounting for the customer's perspective. A sushi bar that advertises high-end omakase experiences but offers an outdated, generic online reservation system risks confusing or frustrating potential diners. **Ensuring that every element of the customer's journey—from ad to table—reflects the campaign's intent reinforces its effectiveness and builds trust with the audience.**

Finally, revisiting and refining goals regularly helps businesses adapt to changing circumstances. A pizzeria might initially aim to grow online orders but later discover a surge in in-person dining interest following a local event. Pivoting the campaign to feature dine-in specials ensures the strategy remains relevant and aligned with emerging trends. This flexibility allows businesses to maximize returns without losing sight of their overarching objectives.

By prioritizing alignment between goals and campaigns, businesses not only increase the effectiveness of their marketing efforts but also create a cohesive narrative that resonates with their audience. This approach transforms marketing from a collection of disconnected tactics into a strategic tool for sustained growth. Through clear objectives, tailored strategies, and consistent evaluation, businesses can ensure their campaigns deliver results that matter.

Overlooking Customer Feedback

"What you measure is what you improve." This quote, often attributed to management expert Peter Drucker, captures the essence of customer feedback's role in shaping successful marketing and operations. Businesses thrive or falter not only on the quality of their products but on how well they listen to the people they serve. For restaurants, where experience is as much the product as the food, ignoring feedback is a shortcut to stagnation. The best ideas often come not from behind the scenes but from the dining room floor.

Consider once again the case of Union Square Hospitality Group, led by restaurateur Danny Meyer, as chronicled in *Setting the Table*. Meyer's philosophy emphasizes the importance of both staff and customer feedback in building a lasting brand. In one example, his team noticed that repeat guests frequently ordered the same dishes, often requesting slight modifications. By listening and adapting, they created a more flexible menu that felt personalized to their diners. This approach didn't just increase satisfaction; it led to higher revenue as customers felt heard and valued. **Feedback is not just commentary; it is an opportunity for innovation.**

The failure to prioritize feedback can lead to marketing campaigns that miss their mark entirely. Imagine a trendy café that spends thousands on promoting a new brunch special without considering customer preferences. If the café's core audience consistently mentions longer wait times as a pain point in reviews, then adding more traffic to the busiest hours only worsens the problem. **Effective feedback collection ensures that marketing efforts address real needs instead of amplifying existing frustrations.**

Collecting feedback requires more than placing a suggestion box by the door. Successful businesses create systems to gather insights in real time, using tools like customer satisfaction surveys, online reviews, and direct conversations. For example, a bakery noticing consistent feedback about the lack of gluten-free options might explore adding those items, especially if customers explicitly mention they would buy them. Platforms like Google My Business and Yelp provide insights into trends, such as which dishes generate the most praise or which complaints are recurring. **These insights should guide not only product decisions but also how those products are marketed to resonate with customers.**

Acting on feedback is where many businesses falter. Gathering information without addressing it creates a perception of indifference that can erode trust. A neighborhood pizzeria that sees repeated complaints about late delivery times cannot afford to ignore the issue. Instead, they could use this feedback to restructure their operations, optimize delivery routes, or even communicate more transparently with customers about expected wait times. Following up with customers to share these changes can transform critics into loyal advocates.

Examples abound of businesses turning criticism into success. Starbucks' decision to implement mobile ordering was a direct response to feedback about long in-store wait times. By creating a system that allowed customers to order ahead, the company addressed their pain point while also opening up a new channel for sales. Similarly, a small fine-dining restaurant in New York began offering a seasonal vegetarian tasting menu after observing feedback from guests who felt overlooked by the regular offerings. Both examples illustrate how responding to feedback not only solves immediate problems but creates new opportunities for growth.

Listening also extends beyond external feedback. The staff's insights are equally vital. Frontline employees are often the first to hear what customers like or dislike, yet their input is frequently overlooked in decision-making. A bustling seafood restaurant might learn from its servers that customers find certain menu descriptions confusing. Incorporating staff suggestions to clarify the language could improve both ordering efficiency and diner satisfaction. **When businesses value internal feedback, they foster a culture of ownership and engagement that translates into better customer experiences.**

Constructive criticism is especially valuable because it highlights areas for improvement that might otherwise go unnoticed. A dessert shop might initially resist suggestions to simplify its menu, fearing it could alienate customers. Yet after reviewing feedback and experimenting with a more focused selection, the shop could find that streamlined offerings enhance both operational efficiency and customer satisfaction. **The willingness to act on difficult feedback separates businesses that adapt and grow from those that stagnate.**

Feedback systems should be integrated into every aspect of marketing and operations. A restaurant promoting a new loyalty program could track customer responses at every touchpoint, from sign-ups to rewards redemption. If data shows low engagement with certain rewards, adjusting the offerings to align with customer preferences ensures that the program delivers real value. Similarly, monitoring feedback after launching a campaign for a new dish might reveal that diners love the concept but find the portion size lacking. Adjusting the execution demonstrates responsiveness and commitment to improvement.

Ultimately, overlooking customer feedback is a risk no business can afford. Beyond providing a window into customer preferences, feedback is a roadmap for avoiding missteps and uncovering new opportunities. By actively listening, responding thoughtfully, and integrating insights into marketing strategies, businesses create stronger connections with their audience and build a foundation for sustained growth. Feedback, when embraced as a partnership with the customer, becomes an invaluable tool for aligning every decision with what truly matters.

Neglecting Branding Consistency

"Consistency is what transforms average into excellence." This quote from business author Tony Robbins encapsulates the critical role branding consistency plays in shaping a successful restaurant business. Imagine stepping into a trendy café with minimalist decor and curated playlists, only to receive a paper menu covered in outdated fonts and a social media page cluttered with mismatched imagery. The disconnect confuses customers and undermines the carefully crafted identity the café intended to project. Branding inconsistency doesn't just dilute a message; it erodes trust.

Strong branding creates a sense of familiarity that customers rely on. When a business maintains a consistent visual and verbal identity, it reassures its audience, signaling professionalism and reliability. A local bakery known for whimsical designs and pastel colors should carry that same aesthetic across its packaging, website, and even email marketing campaigns. **Every point of interaction, from the physical storefront to**

digital platforms, should feel like part of the same cohesive experience. This consistency not only strengthens the brand but also helps it stand out in a crowded market.

Inconsistent branding often stems from unclear guidelines or a lack of oversight. For example, a family-owned barbecue joint might design a modern logo to appeal to younger diners but forget to update its physical signage, which still reflects its rustic roots. This misalignment sends conflicting messages about the business's identity. **A brand should evolve thoughtfully, ensuring that every update complements rather than clashes with its existing image.**

Maintaining uniformity across platforms requires intentional effort. Start by defining the core elements of your brand—colors, fonts, logo usage, and tone of voice. A casual burger spot might choose vibrant colors and playful language, while a high-end sushi restaurant opts for muted tones and refined phrasing. **Once established, these elements should be documented in a brand style guide, a resource that ensures every piece of content aligns with the business's identity.**

Digital tools can help enforce consistency. Platforms like Canva or Adobe Express allow teams to create templates for social media posts, menus, and email newsletters, all adhering to the brand's visual guidelines. Scheduling tools like Hootsuite can help streamline content posting, ensuring that messaging is not only consistent in appearance but also aligned in timing and tone. For instance, if a restaurant is known for family-friendly vibes, promoting late-night cocktail specials might feel out of place unless framed within its broader brand story.

Case studies highlight the power of branding done right. Chipotle, for example, consistently pairs its sleek, modern packaging with messaging about fresh ingredients and ethical sourcing. The alignment between what the customer sees and what the brand stands for builds trust. Similarly, Starbucks excels at creating a unified experience, whether a customer visits a store in Seattle or Tokyo. The logo, menu layout, and even the store's scent work together to reinforce a single, recognizable identity.

Neglecting consistency, on the other hand, risks alienating customers. A Mediterranean bistro that mixes casual Instagram ads with overly formal website copy might confuse diners about what to expect. When branding appears disjointed, it creates uncertainty—customers may wonder if the business has changed ownership, lowered quality standards, or lacks focus. **Consistency acts as a promise, and every inconsistency chips away at that promise.**

Feedback is a valuable tool for identifying gaps in branding. Customers often notice inconsistencies that the business might overlook. For example, a popular pizzeria might receive comments about its hard-to-read menu on mobile devices, suggesting that its design doesn't translate well across formats. Listening to this feedback and making adjustments ensures that branding remains cohesive, no matter the medium.

Training staff to embody the brand's identity is another crucial aspect. A modern health food café with a focus on sustainability can't afford to have team members using plastic bags or providing contradictory information about sourcing practices. **Employees are often the face of the brand, and their actions must align with the brand's values.** Providing training sessions and clear guidelines ensures consistency in both messaging and behavior.

Lastly, review branding regularly to ensure it remains relevant. Businesses evolve, and branding should too, but always in a way that feels deliberate and connected to the original identity. A seafood shack transitioning into a more upscale dining experience might retain its nautical theme but update its logo and menu to reflect the change. **Thoughtful rebranding acknowl-**

edges the past while embracing the future, ensuring that the brand's core remains intact.

Branding consistency isn't just about aesthetics; it's about creating a seamless, trustworthy experience that resonates with customers at every touchpoint. A unified brand communicates confidence and care, helping businesses not only attract customers but also retain them. Through clarity, intentionality, and regular evaluation, businesses can build an identity that feels authentic and enduring, standing out in a world that often feels noisy and fragmented.

Application of Techniques: Avoiding Common Marketing Mistakes

Recognizing and Avoiding Common Marketing Mistakes:

This section provides a robust framework to identify and prevent marketing errors that can erode a brand's reputation, drain resources, and hinder growth. One of the central themes is the importance of grounding marketing decisions in **insights rather than assumptions**. For instance, a small café may believe offering steep discounts will increase foot traffic, only to find it attracts one-time bargain hunters rather than loyal customers. This highlights the importance of using data to validate assumptions before implementing strategies.

Another critical takeaway is **contingency planning**. Imagine a bakery running a promotional campaign for a new dessert that unexpectedly goes viral. Without sufficient preparation, they could run out of stock, leading to disappointed customers and tarnished trust. Businesses should forecast potential outcomes and prepare solutions for various scenarios to avoid turning a successful campaign into a misstep.

Effective tracking and measuring of efforts are also emphasized as a safeguard against wasteful spending. For example, a restaurant might prioritize posting on social media, only to discover through analytics that email campaigns yield higher engagement and revenue. Businesses should regularly evaluate their marketing efforts using tools like Google Analytics or CRM platforms to ensure alignment with their objectives.

Maintaining Branding Consistency: Consistent branding across platforms creates a unified customer experience, fostering trust and recognition. A key application is developing a **brand style guide** that documents colors, fonts, logos, tone, and messaging strategies. This ensures all marketing materials— digital and physical—present a cohesive identity. For instance, a high-end sushi restaurant should maintain its refined aesthetic not only on its menu but also in social media posts and email campaigns.

Incorporating Feedback into Strategy: Listening to customers and staff is crucial for avoiding errors and refining operations. Tools like online review platforms, surveys, and direct feedback channels allow businesses to gather actionable insights. For example, a pizzeria noticing consistent complaints about late delivery times can use this feedback to optimize delivery processes or adjust customer expectations with clearer communication.

Acting on feedback involves visible changes that address customer concerns. For instance, if diners consistently mention a lack of vegetarian options, adding a dedicated vegetarian menu signals responsiveness and builds goodwill. Similarly, involving staff in decision-making fosters internal alignment, ensuring that the brand's promises are reflected in everyday operations.

Action Items

Validate Assumptions with Data:

- Identify any assumptions about your audience or marketing channels.
- Use analytics tools (e.g., Google Analytics, customer surveys) to confirm whether these assumptions align with actual customer behavior.

Develop a Contingency Plan for Campaigns:

- Identify risks associated with your marketing strategies (e.g., increased demand, negative responses).
- Create a plan for addressing each risk, such as stockpiling inventory or pre-training staff.

Track and Measure Campaign Effectiveness:

- Set clear, measurable goals for each campaign (e.g., "Increase weekday reservations by 15%").
- Monitor performance using tools like CRM software or social media analytics.
- Adjust campaigns based on data insights, ensuring alignment with objectives.

Create and Enforce a Brand Style Guide:

- Document brand elements such as logo usage, color schemes, fonts, and tone of voice.
- Share the guide with your team to ensure all marketing materials align with your brand identity.
- Regularly review the guide to ensure relevance and consistency across platforms.

Integrate Feedback into Operations:

- Use surveys, online reviews, and direct conversations to gather feedback.
- Analyze feedback to identify recurring themes or concerns.
- Implement changes based on feedback, such as menu updates, operational adjustments, or targeted marketing strategies.

Train Staff on Brand Alignment:

- Host regular training sessions to ensure employees understand the brand's values and messaging.
- Encourage staff to provide input on customer preferences or operational challenges.

Monitor and Adapt Branding:

- Regularly audit marketing materials and digital platforms for consistency.
- Update branding elements when evolving your identity, ensuring all platforms reflect the change.

Focus on Relevant Metrics:

- Identify metrics directly tied to your goals (e.g., conversion rates for promotional campaigns, click-through rates for ads).
- Avoid "vanity metrics" like likes or impressions that do not correlate with tangible outcomes.

Resource List

Tools:

- **Google Analytics:** Tracks website performance, including traffic sources and user behavior, to evaluate the effectiveness of campaigns.
- **Hootsuite:** Schedules and monitors social media posts to maintain consistent branding and engagement.
- **Canva or Adobe Express:** Provides templates for marketing materials that adhere to brand guidelines.
- **SurveyMonkey:** Collects customer feedback through surveys, offering insights into preferences and pain points.
- **CRM Platforms (e.g., HubSpot, Salesforce):** Tracks customer interactions and campaign effectiveness, ensuring data-driven decision-making.

Books and Articles:

- *Setting the Table* by Danny Meyer
- *Building a StoryBrand* by Donald Miller

CONCLUSION

Marketing is a puzzle where every piece matters, and in the restaurant business, each decision you make has the power to shape not only your bottom line but your story. Throughout this book, we've explored the intricate connections between strategy, creativity, and execution, each vital to building a restaurant that doesn't just exist but thrives. At its heart, marketing isn't a separate part of your business—it's the expression of who you are, what you offer, and why customers should choose you over the countless options vying for their attention.

Every restaurant is unique, but the challenges you face are universal. Whether you're running a cozy family diner or a sleek, modern bistro, the rules of marketing are surprisingly consistent. It starts with understanding your audience—truly knowing the people who walk through your doors or browse your menu online. Their preferences, habits, and expectations form the foundation of every successful campaign. Too often, businesses jump into flashy promotions or trendy platforms without asking the most important question: does this resonate with the people I want to serve? Without that clarity, even the most creative efforts risk falling flat.

Equally essential is the role of your brand. Think of it as the personality of your restaurant, the story that ties together your menu, décor, and interactions with customers. A well-defined brand isn't just about aesthetics—it's a promise. It tells your customers what they can expect from you and ensures that their experience matches their expectations. From your logo to your tone of voice, consistency builds trust. A high-end steakhouse with whimsical social media posts may entertain, but it risks sending mixed signals. Aligning every touchpoint with your brand ensures clarity and keeps your message unmistakable.

One of the most overlooked aspects of restaurant marketing is the value of reflection. Measuring success isn't glamorous, but it's where real growth happens. Data tells a story, revealing what's working, what isn't, and where untapped opportunities lie. Without it, you might find yourself repeating campaigns that don't drive results or overlooking strategies that could transform your business. The bakery that learns its email campaigns perform better than its social media posts gains a competitive edge by focusing resources where they matter most.

It's easy to be swept up in trends or feel pressured to outspend competitors, but some of the most impactful marketing moves are grounded in simplicity and authenticity. Listening to feedback, for instance, is a powerful yet underused tool. Customers often provide a roadmap to success if you're willing to listen. A small café that consistently hears requests for dairy-free options can turn those comments into an opportunity, creating a niche that attracts loyal, appreciative diners. Feedback isn't criticism; it's insight.

Avoiding pitfalls is just as critical as chasing success. Common missteps, like failing to set measurable goals or misaligning campaigns with objectives, waste not only resources but time. Worse, they can damage your reputation. Overpromising and underdelivering leaves customers disappointed, while inconsistent branding creates confusion. The restaurants that thrive are the ones that pause to ask, "What are we trying to achieve, and how does this campaign help us get there?"

The menu itself—often an afterthought—is one of your most effective marketing tools. It's more than a list of items; it's an invitation. Strategic design highlights your most profitable dishes, while compelling descriptions spark curiosity and appetite. Seasonal menus or limited-time offers create excitement, encouraging diners to return again and again. Every detail of your menu, from layout to language, should reinforce your brand and draw customers deeper into the experience.

Through all of this, it's important to remember that marketing isn't about perfection; it's about connection. It's the way you build relationships with your customers, turning first-time visitors into loyal advocates. Whether through a thoughtfully crafted loyalty program, shareable experiences, or simply being a consistent presence in their lives, your goal is to make people feel not just fed but valued.

If there's one takeaway from this journey, it's that marketing is both an art and a discipline. It requires creativity, yes, but also structure, reflection, and a willingness to adapt. By combining these elements, you can create a marketing strategy that not only attracts customers but keeps them coming back, building a business that stands the test of time. This isn't just about selling meals; it's about creating moments that matter, one plate at a time.

Turn casual diners into loyal fans with Do Social Smarter's proven system to grow your customer base, boost reviews, and drive foot traffic effortlessly.

Visit DoSocialSmarter.com today and discover how to keep your seats full and your competition behind.